So What Do They Really Know?

Assessment That Informs Teaching and Learning

Cris Tovani

Stenhouse Publishers
Portland, Maine

Pembroke Publishers
Markham, Ontario

Stenhouse Publishers
www.stenhouse.com

Pembroke Publishers
www.pembrokepublishers.com

Credits
Page 75: "Defiant Teenager Gets Jail Time in Vehicular Homicide," by Monte Whaley. *Denver Post*, September 8, 2004. Reprinted with permission.
Page 79: "Separated from Family: With Parents Deported, San Eli Student Must Fend for Himself," by Aileen B. Flores. *El Paso Times*, September 21, 2010. Reprinted with permission.
Pages 91, 92: Excerpt from *The Great Gatsby*: Reprinted with the permission of Scribner, a Division of Simon & Schuster, Inc., from *The Great Gatsby* (Authorized Text) by F. Scott Fitzgerald. Copyright © 1925 by Charles Scribner's Sons. Copyright renewed © 1953 by Frances Scott Fitzgerald Lanahan. All rights reserved.

Library of Congress Cataloging-in-Publication Data
Tovani, Cris.
    So what do they really know? : assessment that informs teaching and learning / Cris Tovani.
        p. cm.
    Includes bibliographical references.
    ISBN 978-1-57110-730-5 (pbk. : alk. paper)—ISBN 978-1-57110-918-7 (e-book)
1. Education—Evaluation. 2. Educational tests and measurements. 3. Effective teaching. 4. Teacher-student relationships. 5. Academic achievement. I. Title.
    LB1775.T68 2011
    371.26'2—dc22
                                                                        2011011149

Cover design, interior design, and typesetting by Martha Drury
Manufactured in the United States of America

PRINTED ON 30% PCW
RECYCLED PAPER

17 16 15 14 13 12 11   9 8 7 6 5 4 3 2 1

For Kenny, the middle of our center

Contents

Acknowledgments

I started this book five years ago—about the same time that my brother Kenny had received another diagnosis of melanoma. Kenny died May 1, 2009. A month after his death, I found myself making excuses to an editor that I just wasn't up to writing a foreword, as I had promised. I whimpered that my brother had just died and I was too upset to think clearly. The editor sympathetically told me she understood—and just like that, I was off the hook.

As soon as I hung up the phone, I had an overwhelming sensation of my brother's presence. Kenny was shaking his head and saying, "Pull yourself together and quit blaming me for your writer's block. It's time for you to get back to work on that book." And with that, I again started writing. Watching my brother's battle with cancer, and his determination to beat it, inspired me to keep writing. This was a tough book to finish because the field of assessment is changing daily. Every day teachers are faced with the challenge of equitably translating thinking into a grade. They also strive to use assessment in a way that informs their instruction. This book only begins to scratch the surface, and, like the other two books I've written, I couldn't have done it without lots of help.

I thank Kenny for sitting on my shoulder and nudging me through the tough parts. This one is for you, buddy.

I thank my husband, Pete, for being "there" when I couldn't be. I love you. I also thank my daughter Caroline, who stood shoulder to shoulder with me during the most difficult time of my life. You are a lot stronger than you think, and I love you to pieces.

I thank my editor, Philippa, who possesses just the right amount of intuition to know when to push and when to encourage. Her wisdom and patience come in epic proportions. I am humbled and grateful that she lets me take credit for the many good ideas she sends my way.

And last but not least, I thank my friend Samantha Bennett. Without her hours of endless editing, I would still be bumbling around rewriting the same chapters over and over again. Years ago when Sam started facilitating labs in my classroom, I had no idea she'd become my instructional coach and then my dear friend. Her brilliance pushes me every day to rethink what matters most for kids. She makes me laugh and reminds me to take time to "smell the roses." Without her, I'd still be grumpy and stuck.

CHAPTER 1

Assessment: It Doesn't Have to Be the Enemy

We use the general term *assessment* to refer to all those activities undertaken by teachers—and by their students in assessing themselves—that provide information to be used as feedback to modify teaching and learning activities. Such assessment becomes formative assessment when the evidence is actually used to adapt the teaching to meet student needs.

—*Paul Black and Dylan Wiliam (1998)*

Never, in a million years, did I think I would write a book on assessment. But when No Child Left Behind (NCLB) hit its stride, the political tenor got to be too much for me. Its penchant for the business adage, "You manage what you measure," had gone overboard. Instead of NCLB improving teaching and learning, it had morphed into a way to judge and rank kids and teachers.

Thankfully, my elementary roots reminded me why assessment was important in the first place. I realized that assessment wasn't the enemy; it was the way it was being used to *judge and punish* instead of *inform and help* educators get smarter about teaching and learning.

I began to examine my definition of assessment and embrace it in a way that would not only inform my instruction but also provide useful feedback to students. I knew there needed to be multiple pieces of evidence to tell me the stories of the learners in my room so that neither they nor I would ever be judged solely by a test score.

I dug into the reams of research on formative assessment and became intrigued with the thinking of Dylan Wiliam, Paul Black, Grant Wiggins, Jay McTighe, Lorna Earl, Robert Marzano, Susan Brookhart, Ken O'Connor, Mike Schmoker, Rick Wormeli, and Rick Stiggins. I took some risks of my own and realized the possibilities of positive uses of assessment for my students. This book invites readers back into my classroom. But beware: you will not find tips, tricks, or an appendix of formative assessments. My hope is that teachers will recognize that many of the tools they already use, when given a slight tweak, can serve as powerful assessments that will inform instruction and improve achievement. Join me as we try to figure out, "So, what do they *really* know?"

Bombing a Test Doesn't Mean You're Stupid

I've never liked the word *test*. When I was a student, tests never reflected what I thought I knew. Sometimes I'd get a high percentage correct when in my heart I knew I hadn't mastered the material. Other times when I was sure I knew the material, my score would be surprisingly low. I wondered how many of my students felt the same way.

After my class of struggling readers has finished the three days of state testing, I ask how they did. Several of them chuckle and say, "Probably not very good. I didn't even try." I shake my head in frustration and decide to collect a bit of my own data. Instead of picking up where we left off before the testing, I ask students to get out a piece of paper and respond to the following question:

Describe yourself as a test-taker. When are tests hard for you, and what do the results say about you as a learner?

As students dive into the writing, I head over to see what Erik has written. He is by far the best reader in the class and very smart, and the only reason he's in a reading support class is that he refuses to take placement tests seriously. Erik is also honest. He writes, "Tests say very little about me because I never really try on them. Teachers should base kids' classes on other stuff." I nod and move over to see what Vinnie has written.

Vinnie reminds me that sometimes effort is affected by factors outside the school's control. He scribbles, "When I take my medicine, I do better. I can focus and last longer."

Peering over his shoulder, reading what he writes, I ask him, "How do you decide when you are going to take your meds?"

"It's starting to become a habit now," he says. "My mom doesn't even have to ask me to take them anymore. I just want to prove to my parents how smart I am, and I want to get a car." I smile at Vinnie and tell him how strategic he is to use his competitive nature as a motivator.

Wandering over to Vanessa's desk I see that she has written quite a bit. I kneel down to read what is on her paper. She stops writing and looks at me. "I'm a real bad test-taker. When I take tests, I get all nervous, and I start trying to answer the questions really fast just to get done. Then sometimes I accidentally bubble-in the wrong place, and I get worried that I will fail the test. Then I feel all dumb."

"Vanessa," I whisper. "Would it be better to do a few questions right than to rush through and miss a whole bunch?"

"I don't know," she says. "I never thought about that because I don't really think about the questions when I test. I just think about hurrying up and getting it over with."

"Hmm, I wonder if you miss things you know because you are in a hurry."

She looks at the ground. "Yeah, probably, but I don't know."

I have time to touch base with one more student before moving on. I head over to Lauren. She is finished and sitting quietly at her desk. I look at her paper and read, "Tests show that I don't learn a thing. Most of the tests I take, I fail. I don't bother to study anymore because I know I won't remember what I just studied. I have a bad memory so I don't waste my time."

I tell Lauren that in my opinion, she has learned a lot. I point out that at the beginning of the year when she got stuck in her reading, she would just stop and say, "This is boring." Now she is asking questions to isolate her confusion. She has read three books since the beginning of second semester, and two of them she understood so well that she recommended them to other students in the class. I point out that she can now read for forty minutes without stopping and that her annotations have gotten so good that she is often the leader of her discussion group.

I can tell Lauren is pleased and surprised by what I have just told her. I'm not sure she believes me, though, because she says, "Well, I don't know if I've gotten smarter. I do know that if teachers really go by what my test scores say, I would look like I never learn anything even though I work hard."

Acing a Test Doesn't Mean You "Get It"

Picture the scene. In late June, 250 teachers gather in Denver to attend the Rocky Mountain Reading Conference. During the afternoon breakout sessions, thirty teachers join me to discuss assessment. I pass out a student work sample from my senior English class. It's a summative assessment designed to measure how well students have learned forty-five vocabulary words. The sample I share is a perfect paper, without a single error.

All participants get a copy of the multiple-choice, fill-in-the-blank test and are asked to examine it and share what they think they can tell about the student who is responsible for the work.

"He's obviously a good student," responds one teacher.

"He studies hard," says another. As teachers throw out responses, I record them on a sheet of chart paper.

"Yes, I think this student cares about school."

"I think he has a good command of the English language," volunteers another.

I smile with each response. I know the point I was hoping to make will be made with this example. After a few more responses, the remarks taper off. Rather quickly, it seems, teachers have run out of things to say.

I pass out another sample. This one, however, is not a perfect paper. It's sparse in thinking and hard to read because of poor handwriting and misspellings. However, this sample differs in that it is a formative assessment. Instead of a vocabulary test, participants examine an inner-voice sheet (see Figure 1.1; a blank version of this form is included in the appendix). On this sample, the student has been asked to record his thinking as he reads several pages from Mitch Albom's book *The Five People You Meet in Heaven*.

When participants start to share what they can tell about this student, their responses are not as glowing.

"This kid isn't a very good writer," says a teacher in the back.

Defensively, his tablemate says, "He might not be a native English-speaker."

"I don't think he likes to write, but I think he has understood this part of the book."

"Yes, I think he is also thinking about his life and making connections to it and the book."

"He's also making predictions. He thinks the wife will be someone Eddie meets at the end."

"It sounds to me like he has some issues with his dad."

"Maybe he's just being a regular eighteen-year-old."

Figure 1.1
Inner-Voice Sheet

Name Fara F.
Period
Date

INNER-VOICE SHEET

Title of Book The Five People You Meet in Heaven

Author of Book Mitch Albom

Directions: Begin reading on page ___91___. Record the conversation you have in your head as you read. Be sure to have **at least four (4) sentences per box**. If you catch yourself using a reading strategy, add that at the bottom of the box. Also decide if the conversation inside your head distracts you from making meaning or if the voice helps you interact with the text.

Inner Voice on page ___92___	Inner Voice on page ___96___
That thing on Adam and eve thing was cool did he really know what to do when he was put on this world. When you die people are waiting does that mean who is there for those people.	The captain was there to give him somthin to remember the girl that Eddie was in love with. What happens to her and does He meet her? I think he did save the girl.

Inner Voice on page ___101___	Inner Voice on page ___110___
Why was eddie farther so hard on him. I guess thats how dads are My dad is hard on me because he dosent want to be like him when I have a family of my own.	When it said all family damage their kids could be true. My family has helped me the most but has hurt me the worst too.

The comments continue. It's clear that the group can tell a lot more about this student from the inner-voice sheet than they could from the multiple-choice, fill-in-the-blank vocabulary test that they examined first. I let the group speculate for a few more minutes, and then I share that they have just examined the work of the same student. Teachers are shocked. "How could the same student have such different performances?" some ask. It's a great question.

I flash back to the day a month earlier when I gave the vocabulary test. This was not a typical day for me, because I was conducting research. Usually the desks are arranged in tables of four or five, but before school started, I moved all the desks out of their pods and put them in neat rows with lots of aisle space. Seldom if ever do I give multiple-choice, fill-in-the-blank tests. But today, I wanted to see if students' performance on this test would match my knowledge of their word mastery. Could I accurately assess how well students had learned their vocabulary words using this kind of measurement?

To test this hypothesis, I had to rule out as much cheating as possible, so during the test, I planned to walk up and down rows so that I could eagle-eye each student. I'd stapled the test pages out of order so that if by chance someone did try to look at another person's test, it would be confusing. I wanted to do everything I could to control the variables that might affect my little experiment. As I patrolled the room, I searched for definitions written on desktops that might serve as impromptu crib sheets. All notebooks were safely stored in backpacks and cell phones were out of sight.

There was one student in particular that I planned to watch out for. If anyone were going to cheat, it would be this kid. Sure enough, it wasn't two minutes into the test before I had to bark, "Faraz, eyes on your own paper."

Defensively, he said, "I'm not looking. No one by me even has the same test." I chuckled to myself. Within the first few minutes, Faraz had already figured out that I'd made multiple versions of the test and had strategically passed them out so that no one would have a test like his or her neighbor's.

After school, I quickly graded the assessment and thought, *No wonder some people love these kinds of tests.* They take no time at all to grade. As a matter of fact, it took longer to sort the tests into piles and make different answer keys for each version than it did to actually do the grading. I did Ashley's first. She earned a 94 percent—no surprise. Dominique scored a 54 percent—no surprise there either. Patrick earned an 80 percent, which sounded right. I blasted through five more tests until finally getting to Faraz's. He aced the first page. He did the same thing on the second page, then the third. In disbelief, I scanned the fourth page only to discover that he had earned 100 percent! I was shocked, stupefied, and itching to find out how he had done it. I stopped grading, put down the pen, and tried to picture what Faraz was doing during the test. I had watched him like a hawk! I hadn't seen him cheat, but I knew there was no way he could get 100 percent without cheating. On the way home from school, I couldn't get Faraz out of my head.

Student Responses to a Class-Opening Prompt

Why do you cheat?

- "I don't care about what I'm learning. So I don't study, but I do want to get a good grade, so I copy someone or cheat to get the grade."
- "There are so many expectations placed on me about getting good grades. I don't want to disappoint my parents."
- "Sometimes it takes too long to learn something that I don't really care about. I just cheat to get it over with."
- "I cheat so I don't have to think."
- "There is too much meaningless information to memorize."
- "I cheat when I don't care about the class."
- "I cheat so I'm not embarrassed."
                    —*2010 Senior Class*

I know Faraz well. He's been a student of mine on and off since ninth grade. He came to the United States from Syria when he was in elementary school. He speaks English well without an accent but struggles to read and write. He is very Americanized, and there is no way to tell by his dress or appearance that he isn't American born.

His freshman year in my Reading Essentials class, he was a struggling reader who hated teachers, books, and anything that had to do with school. We had a good year together, and he took my Reading Essentials II class as a sophomore. He didn't flunk, but was still several years below grade level when it came to reading and writing. I didn't have Faraz as a junior, but he visited often. We would talk about music. He was fascinated by 1960s bands, and I had given him a few biographies to read on his own. At times Faraz would come into my office to share with me arguments he had had with his father, who was worried that he was going to end up in jail because he didn't act like his Syrian cousins who followed more traditional ways.

In the fall of his senior year, Faraz told me that he had signed up to take College Prep English 12 with me second semester. "Great," I said, "but you better be ready to work. There is homework every night. You'll have to read and do lots of writing." Faraz wasn't worried. He knew that if he came to class and worked hard, I'd work with him.

All spring he was conscientious about doing most of his assignments. The only aspect of the class where Faraz refused to participate was the vocabulary study. He hated the weekly word lists and quizzes. I offered to accept late work with a penalty. Faraz ignored my attempts to help him do the vocabulary activities in his notebook, and on Fridays he'd come late to class so that he'd miss the weekly quiz. Instead of making it up, he took the zero. He even went so far as to average his grade to figure out how many zeros he could get and still pass with a C. It was clear that Faraz didn't care about vocabulary and wasn't going to play the game.

I couldn't get Faraz out of my mind on the drive home that day. I knew there was no way he would have studied enough to memorize the words for this test. I also knew that if he didn't do well on it, he would get a D in the class. For Faraz, this was a high-stakes assessment. So when he got 100 percent on the vocabulary test, I knew he had cheated. I just didn't know how.

The next day, Faraz met me at my office door and asked if I'd graded the vocabulary tests. I could tell he was anxious. Unlocking the door, I laughed and said, "Yeah, and you flunked."

"That's impossible," he said. "There is no way I flunked. Are you sure you used the right answer key when you graded mine?"

"Yes, Faraz, I'm sure." I looked him in the eye and asked, "Why would you think you passed the test, let alone earned an A, when you didn't do the weekly work? You didn't even look at the words on the review, let alone learn them."

Panicking a bit he said, "Tovani, there is no way I could have failed."

"And why is that, Faraz? Did you cheat?" Faraz didn't say a word. He only smiled. "Actually, Faraz, you got 100 percent. Seriously, how did you do it?"

"Do what?" he asked.

"How did you get the A?"

Slyly he said, "I studied."

I said, rudely, "You lie."

Gloating he said, "You're right."

"So you cheated?" I asked.

"Heck, yeah. How'd you think I got 100 percent?"

Having him right where I wanted him, I said, "Well, I guess I have to turn you in to the dean."

Color drained from his face, and he said, "Turn me in? You can't turn me in. I'll fail your class, and then I won't graduate. My dad will kill me."

After a bit of begging and lots of negotiating, Faraz and I came to an agreement. He promised to tell me how he cheated, and I promised not to notify the dean.

Almost bragging, Faraz told me how he did it. "I gave my friend the list of vocabulary words. When I didn't know a word, which was most of the time, I would text him the word and then he would text me back the definition."

"But I was watching you."

"I know. You almost caught me once."

"But didn't it take forever to get the answers?"

"Not really. I text-message all the time, so my fingers move really fast. I don't even have to look at the keyboard when I do it." Worried that I'd go back on my promise, he asked, "You're not going to turn me in, are you?"

"No," I said. "But you are not getting 100 percent. You'll need to do some vocabulary notebooks to make up the points."

"That's cool," he said. "As long as I pass this class, I'll do it. Thanks, Tovani."

Faraz left my office. I was disappointed that he had cheated, but in a way he confirmed my suspicion. Just because a kid aces a test doesn't mean he knows and understands the material.

Returning to My Assessment Roots

My first ten years of teaching were spent at the elementary level. Back then weeks of school weren't set aside to prepare kids for the state assessment. Recesses weren't cut short, and no one missed art class because they scored below "proficient." During those years, the concept of daily assessment didn't send shivers down my spine. In those days, I actually valued it because it helped me form my instructional groups. It guided the way I addressed individual needs, and it helped students know how to become independent readers. As an elementary teacher, "assessing all the time" was a way of life. It informed my instruction and gave me a way to share information with my students. Simply put, it made me a better teacher.

After teaching ten years at the high school level, I found myself stuck, trying to equate the word *assessment* with *testing*. At the secondary level, it isn't only the annual state test that students are subjected to. There are the "practice" tests that prepare students for the actual ACT and SAT college entrance exams. There are the International Baccalaureate and Advanced Placement tests that help students earn college credit. There are standardized tests that schools use to appropriately place students in English and math classes. There are pretests and chapter tests, final exams and common assessments.

I did everything I could to sabotage the system and downplay "assessment" because these test results showed only a snapshot of each of my students, not a full photo album of their lives as learners. Since they didn't tell the full story, I mostly tried to ignore them.

But even as I tried to ignore them, I began to live in fear of falling test scores in this new culture of "assessment." It wasn't a very scholarly way to approach something that was such a big part of my profession, but putting blinders on helped me keep my focus on kids.

I realized how jaded I'd become when, under my breath, I made a flippant comment about test data at a mandatory meeting. An administrator said to me with an intense look in his eyes, "This data is no joke. Kids' lives depend on these scores. Their entire future could be altered if they don't do well." No, I thought, not *their* future—just mine and yours.

When test scores carry so much weight, it's no wonder teaching and learning take a backseat to test prep. After years of test hysteria, I had grown accustomed to equating the word *assessment* with all things pointless and evil.

I remember the moment I was unwittingly led back to a richer definition. I had just finished demonstrating a reading strategy in front of a group of visiting teachers and was quickly looking through student work to see what I could learn about the students when I heard someone say, "Cris assesses all the time." Surprised by the comment, since I hadn't tested at all, I thought perhaps I hadn't heard correctly.

The lab facilitator asked, "What did you see or hear Cris do that led you to believe she assesses all the time?"

"Well," the teacher said, "I saw Cris ask students at the beginning of the period to write on a sticky note what they did when they got stuck. I also saw her quickly walk around the room to read the sticky notes to see what strategies students could describe. I also heard Cris ask several students to tell her more. She did the same thing when kids started reading and annotating their short texts. Even before the class started, I saw Cris assessing the kids' T-shirts. She read this one kid's shirt and said, 'Oh, so you like the Tar Heels?' As soon as Cris said that, the students didn't look so scared about having all of us in the room. Cris is constantly assessing her students, but in a good way."

Initially the teacher's comment took me aback, but then I realized she was right. I was assessing. I was "reading the room." I was looking at students' faces to see who was tired, who was grumpy, who was excited to be there. I was reading their T-shirts, their ball caps, and their notebooks, trying to find out their interests and passions outside of school. When they started working, I was looking for ways they were making sense of text and trying to name the strategies they were using so they could consciously apply them again. There was no test in sight, yet I was assessing the whole time.

Different Purposes and Audiences for Assessment

In an attempt to reclaim my assessment roots, I jotted down all the different ways I gather information about my students. I noticed that I could sort the information into two different columns (Figure 1.2). The column on the left held assessments that gave me immediate feedback and informed my instruction. The column on the right listed assessments that took place after the teaching and learning was done, but served to rank students and identify trends.

Assessments for Learning: Firsthand Data Sources	Assessments of Learning: Secondhand Data Sources
I can "see" or "hear" this data. It immediately informs my practice and is a venue for giving students feedback. I get to manage and immediately use this data.	I have to work hard to "read and interpret" this data. Often I don't know if I understand it correctly. It may reflect an accurate picture of the learner, but more often than not, it is a snapshot of the learner. Targeting specific needs is difficult because measuring critical thinking is sacrificed in the name of efficient scoring.
<ul><li>conferring notes</li><li>conversation calendars</li><li>annotated text</li><li>double-entry diaries</li><li>students' surveys and responses</li><li>exit tickets*</li><li>inner-voice sheets</li><li>writing samples, drafts over time</li><li>silent-reading response sheets</li><li>work folders</li><li>discussion records</li><li>response journals</li></ul>	<ul><li>state test scores</li><li>SAT scores</li><li>EXPLORE scores</li><li>PLAN scores</li><li>ACT scores</li><li>grades from the previous year or semester</li><li>district writing assessments</li><li>final exams</li><li>chapter quizzes and tests</li></ul>

*Exit ticket: students leave a brief response about what they learned, what they wondered, and/or what they need.

Figure 1.2

Examining the table, I realized that the left-hand side listed formative assessments, and the right-hand side held summative assessments. The informality of the left side was what the experts refer to as assessments *for* learning (Black and Wiliam 1998), whereas those on the right-hand side were more formal and considered to be assessments *of* learning.

Looking at the chart, it became clear to me why teachers and district officials aren't on the same side when it comes to placing value on the data. Each audience has different needs, and depending on the needs, different assessments are valued.

As a classroom teacher, I value the items on the left because they provide immediate feedback and help me assess learning along the way. I don't have to wait for an outsider to score it and then deliver the results, nor do I need a district data coach to interpret how well my students did.

The items on the right side hold more weight with administrators, parents, and college officials—essentially, the power brokers—because these assessments are designed to sort, rank, and neatly distribute students so that their performances can be compared with others.

Unfortunately, the pressure to raise test scores is driving public school officials and teachers to put more stock into numerical data from the right-hand side than the anecdotal data from the left-hand side. It is easy for educators to get lulled into thinking they've done their jobs after they have spent hours analyzing data. However, looking at the numbers is useless if nothing else happens. Asking teachers to use this data the following year is an ill-timed practice, because the horse is already out of the barn. It is too late to improve our former students' achievement. A metaphor I return to again and again is summative assessment as autopsy (Reeves 2000, 2004).

Sure, an autopsy might inform the medical profession, comfort a family member, or provide useful information to a crime investigator, but it doesn't do anything for the person who has died. Like the autopsies, summative assessments can rank and categorize learners, give colleges a way to standardize how they admit prospective students, and allow parents to brag about their genius child. Unfortunately, they don't help students get smarter in the tested area.

With summative assessments, students are left out of the conversation. Rarely do they get to use the results to improve their performance. Summative assessments are too final. They tell the learner, "Time's up. Put your pencils down. If you don't know the information by now, it's too late." There isn't a lot teachers can do for the learners if summative data is available only after students have moved on to another grade level or class.

Recently a district coordinator told me that whenever he even mentions the words *data* and *assessment*, teachers bristle and immediately dismiss him. Perhaps, teachers have become accustomed to the results being used to point out their failings and student weaknesses, instead of as a place from which to start addressing student needs. It is no wonder teachers tune administrators out at the mere mention of the words. Interpreting reams of numerical data is complicated. Only a select few seem to be able to make sense of it. Sadly, even after the results have been deciphered, they're often rendered useless to the average classroom teacher. Figuring out what students know using numerical data has gotten so complicated that schools are now hiring people to be "data coaches."

There isn't a teacher alive who doesn't know there is an achievement gap. The numbers are pretty darn clear in that area. What is not so obvious is how to use the data to close the gaps.

Teachers don't need any more numerical "data." What they need is validation to use the data that matters most—like student work and student talk—to help them figure out next steps for the learners in their educational care.

Formative Assessments Give Teachers Power

I have worked hard to reclaim my original concept of assessment and remember why I valued it in the first place. I constantly question whether my expanded definition of *assessment* will be accepted by those who write my evaluations.

When I began learning about formative assessments, I went to the appendices of my first two books, *I Read It, but I Don't Get It* (2000) and *Do I Really Have to Teach Reading?* (2004). I recognized that almost everything in the appendices were formative assessments. These were tools that I used to help me "see" how students were making sense of text, and they pointed me in the direction of what I needed to teach next.

They also gave students an opportunity to show what they were thinking. Regardless of their skill level, they all could participate in the activity. Students could also practice constructing meaning without worrying about getting the wrong answer. No sheet required that they respond the same way. Instead learners could leave tracks of their thinking so I could adjust my instruction to better meet their needs.

Back to the medical metaphor, formative assessments are like a wellness physical. During checkups, doctors tell patients where they are healthy. They also give patients feedback in areas where they are not so healthy. Good doctors take it a step further and give suggestions for how to improve the conditions that are interfering with the patients' overall health.

Formative assessments help teachers name areas of strengths for students. Teachers can also adjust their instruction and give targeted feedback so that students can improve their performance. Formative assessments nurture hope and say to students, "You might not get this yet, but you will. Here is something else you can try that might help you understand and improve." Formative assessment empowers teachers and students because it gives them specific information about individual performance. When teachers share the information with students, students have a concrete way to improve. Figure 1.3 summarizes some of the major differences between formative and summative assessments.

Teachers have power over formative assessments—the assessments that matter most to learning. I remember the first time I shared this *aha* with an audience. An indignant woman stood up and said, "No ma'am, we don't have power over assessment. In my district we don't get to say word one about it."

I was surprised by her response, so I asked her to tell me more. When she started to describe the assessment she had no control over, I quickly realized that she was referring to summative measurements. She was right. Most of the time she didn't have a say over those. She had to give the state

Figure 1.3 Major Differences Between Formative and Summative Assessments

Qualities of Formative Assessments	Qualities of Summative Assessments
along-the-way, everyday instructional practice	at the end, after learning has occurred, with no chance to redo
daily practice toward a product	product only
immediate feedback for the teacher and learner	feedback for both the teacher and learner often delayed
informs the teacher and the learner so instruction and practice can be adjusted the next day	informs future instruction and course design
focuses on the task; geared toward understanding	focuses on the individual's mastery of information at specific point in time
allows assessor to get and give immediate feedback to improve student achievement	frequently used as a way to sift and sort students for course placement; serves as a gatekeeper for advanced classes and electives

test. In her building she didn't even have a say over common assessments. She had to administer them every quarter whether they were useful or not. Because those in power place more value on summative assessments, she did as well, and started to believe that they were the only ones that carried weight. Like I used to, she was equating assessment only with testing. At the time, I hadn't clearly distinguished for myself what the differences were, so I didn't do much to relieve her frustration. All I could do was sympathize with her, knowing that summative assessments alone couldn't support students and teachers like formative assessments could when it came to daily instruction. Yet we continue to rely on isolated test scores more than we do on the research that cites that formative assessments matter most when it comes to achievement (Black and Wiliam 1998; Earl 2004; Brookhart 2009).

In education, a lot of things are beyond classroom teachers' control. They can't excuse students from high-stakes assessments. They have no say in how large their class sizes are and can't turn students away, even when there are no more empty desks in their room. They are obligated to welcome and teach every student even though they have no control over who does homework or who comes to class. However, they do have control over how they use formative assessment. When formative assessments are given along the way, they help teachers know what students need and also give students ideas on how to improve. They feed teachers and, more important, feed students so they can grow. That is a lot of control, and a lot of power.

As teachers prepare students for this millennium, assessment needs to be localized to the classroom so that it can serve instructional practice and enhance engagement and achievement. Instead of instruction serving state and national assessments, it needs to serve students.

Similar to *I Read It, but I Don't Get It* and *Do I Really Have to Teach Reading?* I have included a section at the end of each chapter in this book labeled "What Works." It is designed to give readers a brief summary of the topics addressed in the chapter. In addition, I added a new structure using a question I often ask my students: "Are you up for a challenge?" Teachers may find this section helpful to reflect on their own practice and to use in professional learning communities or department meetings to discuss and enhance their assessment practice.

What Works

Assessment Point: Effective assessors know that there are many different kinds of assessment. They recognize that no one assessment can measure everything. They decide what they want to assess and then choose the tool that best informs their instruction.

Assessment Point: Effective assessors recognize that assessment has many different audiences. The most useful assessments not only inform instruction but also inform students about their performance. Information gleaned from assessments should be used to affirm strengths as well as shore up areas of needed growth.

"Are You Up for a Challenge?"

1. Write your definition of *assessment.* Remember, the way in which you define assessment will affect how you grade and give feedback. What kind of data informs your instruction? Do you share the data with students? Is data a way to improve students' performance, or is it merely a way to categorize students?

2. Expand your definition of *assessment.* List all the ways you assess your students. Be sure to consider assessments that don't have numerical data attached to them. Which ones help you and which ones help your students? What makes the assessments you value useful, and how can you use them more often?

CHAPTER 2

Let's Get Personal

We must not see any person as an abstraction. Instead we must see within every person a universe with its own secrets, with its own treasures, with its own sources of anguish, and with some measure of triumph.

—*Elie Wiesel (Annas and Grodin 1992)*

I hold true to the belief that to be able to teach my students well, I need to know them well. Believing this is a whole lot easier than actually doing it, especially when teaching seventy-five or more students a day. I use two easy-to-manage techniques that help me get to know my students and figure out what they need. One tool is the conversation calendar from *Do I Really Have to Teach Reading?* (2004), and the other is just asking students specific questions that I am curious about. Sometimes the questions are about their thinking processes. Other times they are about their interests outside of school. These two tools allow me to check in with kids to gauge their mood, interests, and temperament. Often I can quickly read what students have written and, if I choose to, respond to them in a variety of ways that are not pushy or invasive but truly show my interest. Best of all, they help me build relationships and figure out who my students are as people and learners.

Data That Matters: Conversation Calendars

The weekly calendar, as I used to call it, has been renamed the conversation calendar by my students because of the way it lets us "talk back and forth." This is one assessment tool that I use on a regular basis because it gives me data that quickly helps me build a relationship with my students.

Sometimes people are taken aback by its simplicity. Just last spring a teacher observing my classroom said, "I'm surprised that you're still using those." I grabbed the calendars from the tray by the door and handed them to her so she could read what the kids had written. I wanted her to discover just how much information I got from those jam-packed little boxes of writing. After reading a few, she turned to me and said, "Wow, there is a lot here." I didn't say a word. I nodded and smiled. She was right. There was a lot there.

The conversation calendars help me know students in several different ways. When students initially start using them, I discover their likes, dislikes, struggles, and successes. Learning about them in this way gives me empathy so I have patience for students who initially struggle or want to avoid learning. Figure 2.1 shows Jon's calendar from the first week of school (blank versions of conversation calendars are in the appendix). I learn that we share an affinity for football. Our favorite team is the Denver Broncos, and we both think Rod Smith was an amazing player. The second day of school Jon tells me about his visit to jail to see his brother. I can tell Jon loves his brother and worries about him. I am reminded that my students have lives and challenges outside of school that sometimes make learning about grammar and punctuation rules difficult.

As the year progresses, I can begin using the conversation calendars to assess curricular understanding. Sometimes I write an open-ended question on the calendars before I make copies for the class. The question is designed to give me insight into the students' depth of knowledge around the use of a strategy or the mastery of a concept. When I use calendars this way, it is a quick check for me to see what I need to reteach. I am curious to know what students are wondering about, what is confusing them, and what kinds of connections they are making. On this particular week, I want to check in with them to see how they are responding to *Romeo and Juliet* (Figure 2.2).

Colin's calendar responses show that he is working hard to see connections between modern times and the themes of the play. I praise the con-

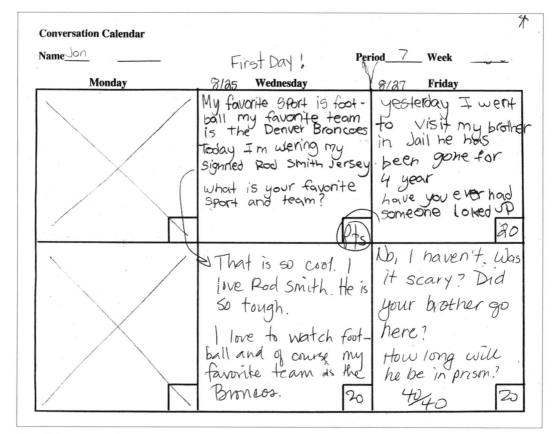

Figure 2.1
Jon's Conversation
Calendar

nection but push to see if he knows what a fatal flaw is. Colin uses his
background knowledge about lacrosse when he writes his response.
Clearly he understands what he is reading and feels some kinship for
Romeo's impulsiveness.

Sometimes the calendars inspire students to write more. They serve as
an outlet for students who are trying to make sense of their lives outside of
school. Most of the time students write only in the upper box.
Occasionally a student writes more. Usually this burst of writing happens
when something distressing or confusing is happening to them. Below is a
poem that Susana wrote. For privacy's sake, I did not include her calendar.
However, she filled up the first box and then went on to fill up the entire
right side and the length of the backside. On this calendar, Susana shares
how immigration officials recently discovered her father. He was running
a successful auto-body shop when his competitors turned him in to U.S.
Immigration Customs Enforcement. He was immediately deported, but
his wife, who was also undocumented, was given a thirty-day extension to

CONVERSATION CALENDAR

NAME: Colin   PERIOD: WEEK OF:

TUESDAY

I need some feedback... Tell me how you are liking the study of Romeo & Juliet. What are you wondering? What is your opinion and what modern day connections do you see? Feel free to go into my space.

I'm liking the study of Romeo and Juliet I'm wondering | 20 | why did Romeo act so quickly when he killed Paris and himself. Why didn't he give himself time to feel bad and if he did she would be awake and they wouldn't be dead. Modern day connections would be that people act quickly when | 20 20 | They don't know what is going on like in lacrosse you take a crazy shot when you are down

THURSDAY

Your connection to today is so good. It's weird how well Shakespeare knew human nature. Romeo was so impulsive. He acted without thinking. I think it was his fatal flaw. Do you know what a fatal flaw is? I think fatal | 20 | flaw means that when you act too quickly it can be fatal. Shakespeare used human nature to his advantage because he knew what people wanted to see and also what people acted like when | 20 | they were in love. He also was timeless with his work and tried to stay away from his day of age things. by one with like 10 seconds and everyone is sad.

Figure 2.2
Colin's Calendar

get her affairs in order. Most likely she was given this reprieve because their children were born in the United States. Susana was able to verbalize her struggle on the calendar, and it inspired her to write for a real reason. She brought this poem to me the next day:

Deportation
by Susana

I'm not a blue-eyed, blond hair
Or a dark-skin black eyed

They say this isn't my home and
To go back to my abandoned house

I know nothing about my great grandmother
Or President George Washington

I speak in a language of two
Not knowing either

Being where I've always been
But never knowing for how long

The INS says that
I don't belong

What do they know about being an immigrant?
What do they know about being an American?

The land of the dreams won't let me sleep
Thinking of deportation.

I asked Susana if I could share her poem to help others see a kid's perspective on immigration. Susana agreed but told me to make sure her last name wasn't on the poem. She worried that someone would come to "get her."

How Calendar Data Helps Me

I teach on a block schedule, which means that I see my students for 100 minutes every other day. The first week of school, I see them three times. During those class periods, I learn a great deal about them from reading their calendars. Figure 2.3 shows a small sampling from the first week of school and what I did with what I learned.

Taking time to know my students through the calendars helps me figure out what they need. Conversation calendars are a fast and easy way to get to know who my students are as individuals. I have a hard time learning from someone who doesn't know or care about me. Students are the same way.

In each of my classes, I work hard to provide what research says are sound instructional practices (Zemelman, Daniels, and Hyde 1998). I give my students ample time and opportunities to engage in authentic reading, writing, and discussing. I model my thinking and provide scaffolding. I search for compelling pieces of text for students to read and write about. However, implementing all the best practices in the world won't make a bit of difference if I don't take time to engage with my students. Teaching them how to become better readers, writers, and thinkers depends upon creating a positive environment where kids are willing to do the work. From the calendars I learn there are a lot of quiet kids. I know right away that I have to start building trust. If the climate in the classroom is not welcoming, positive, and encouraging, I spend the entire class period

Figure 2.3 Calendars as Formative Assessment

What One Week of Calendars Taught Me	How This Data Helps Me Teach Students "Better"
Tessa likes poetry, her favorite book is *A Light in the Attic*, she is terrible at math, and she has an older sister who dropped out of school.	Show Tessa the basket of poetry anthologies. She might need support to stay in school. I want to check in with her other teachers/classes to make sure she doesn't get behind and give up like her sister did.
Joseph likes to draw but not talk in front of the class, his best friend is Alex, and when they sit together, they like to talk, so they don't get much work done.	Don't call on him at first. Pair him with Alex during discussion groups. Separate during work time.
Dominique runs track, hates the hurdles, likes to watch basketball, uses her student planner, likes to be on time, and will read mysteries.	She likes to be organized and on time—let her help me with class routines. Keep an eye out for mysteries she might like to read.
Chris plays freshman football, likes the Broncos, detests the Raiders, and switches vowels when he writes.	Might have an IEP; check with counselor. Clip and bring in current football articles to build fluency, vocabulary, and endurance.
Cheryl put her dog to sleep on Friday, her favorite book is *Twilight*, and she prefers to not talk in class.	Pay attention to her moods, might self-isolate. Don't call on her in front of large group. Introduce her to another vampire series.
Cindy is a tenth grader. She flunked freshman English because she couldn't make first hour because she worked until 11 p.m. helping her parents clean offices. Javier is one of her cousins, but she has so many cousins that she doesn't even know them all.	Find out why Cindy flunked—didn't turn in work or work was too difficult?
Javier likes *futbol*, has three little sisters, and was a class clown in eighth grade but wants to change and be a good student in high school.	Give Javier attention for positive behaviors; quickly catch him doing something well and praise him for it.
José wants to work on computers when he grows up but is really bad at math so he doesn't know if can do it. In his spare time he takes computers apart and puts them back together again.	Put José in contact with the new director of the Science and Technology program.

Figure 2.3 Calendars as Formative Assessment *(continued)*

Daniel is a black belt, doesn't spell well, and wants to improve his vocabulary.	It takes a lot of discipline to be a black belt. Use that to help him develop new vocabulary and spell better.
Kylee likes to seem like she is "bad," but she asks lots of questions on her calendar and appears to be inquisitive.	Find out what she wants to know more about and feed her books on those topics. See if she responds to positive reinforcement.
Chris M. plays football for the school team and likes to scuba dive.	Use football eligibility to reinforce strong study habits during first quarter. Share football articles.
Ricardo babysits his younger brother and sister. His mom doesn't speak English, but he is teaching her, he wants to go into the Air Force, and thinks he could be good at technical drawing.	Put him in touch with Science and Tech program.
Rodrigo was born in Mexico, likes *futbol*, and doesn't like to do group work or talk when school is boring.	Don't let him slip through the cracks. Make sure he has a way to show his thinking nonverbally (sticky note responses, etc.).

managing off-task behaviors. When students know that I am invested in knowing who they are as people, they are more willing to exert the effort necessary to master challenging work.

Just Ask Them

One day, I overheard some of my students bragging about how they had *aced* their test in the previous class without even cracking the book. I was curious to know what they had done so that I could make sure they didn't do the same thing in my class. My eavesdropping didn't yield any clues about how they carried out their scam, so I decided to just come right out and ask them how they had done it. I assured them I would protect their anonymity and that I wouldn't use what they shared to sabotage them. Much to my surprise, they sang like birds.

What they shared gave me a great deal of insight into how they avoided learning. It was the most useful data about learning strategies that I had received in a long time. I was so excited by their responses that I started collecting more questions to ask them. I wanted to know: Why do you cheat? What prevents you from turning in homework? What do you do when you get stuck? Do you fake read? How does what you read in my class connect to other classes? How can I help you? How do you start your writing? How do you write something about a novel when you haven't read the novel? The list of questions went on and on.

Sometimes I pull from the above list of random questions and compile them into surveys. From these surveys I can quickly learn how students manage their time, why they avoid work, how they beat the system, and how they use strategies to negotiate difficulty. The more I learn about the way they learn, or in some cases avoid learning, the more effective I am when it comes to engaging them emotionally and behaviorally.

Following are examples of surveys designed to help me figure out how to best meet the literacy needs of a large class. Even in tracked classes there are students whose abilities and interests vary greatly. I usually give the Beginning of Course Survey (Figure 2.4) the first day of class, and it always gives me insight into behaviors that students use to survive or thrive (at least grade-wise) in school. I am eager to read what students have written, because I learn how kids try to look smart without doing the work. I learn who has metacognitive strategies and who doesn't. I discover what they struggle with, and I get insight into what they are willing and unwilling to do.

Kimberly, an avid reader and the daughter of a colleague, writes on her survey that even though she likes to read, she doesn't do "school reading." She comes right out and says that she doesn't like her teachers' selections so she simply "works around the assignments." On question three she reports that she still manages to get As in her English class even without doing the reading. Question five tells me how she does it. Kimberly writes,

Figure 2.4

Beginning of Course Survey: You as a School Reader

1. List the types of reading or texts that are difficult for you to read. Be as specific as possible.
2. Describe what you do to help yourself when you're having difficulty reading a text. If you automatically quit reading or find a way to get around the reading, explain in detail what you do.
3. What grade did you earn in your last English class?
4. Describe what you were assigned to read in the class and share how much of the reading you actually did.
5. If you didn't do a majority of the reading, describe in detail what you did to get around it.

"SparkNotes are seriously way better than the actual book because they analyze motifs, characters, writing styles, etc." I can almost hear the intonation in her voice as I read her response. She definitely knows "teacher talk" and is probably a pro when it comes to playing the game of school.

It's good to know the very first day of class that Kimberly reads all the time. It's also good to know that she is not going to read what I assign if SparkNotes are available. I have to pique her curiosity and give her a reason to read. I'm challenged by her remarks to show her that there are lots of reasons to read other than for entertainment. I will need to show her how to stay engaged when the reading is difficult or boring. If I don't, I worry she will be betrayed by her SparkNotes trick. Kimberly has to learn how to construct meaning when she encounters text that hasn't been synthesized for her. Many students avoid reading deeply because they aren't sure how to do it with the vast amounts of text they are assigned. They want to get good grades, so they resort to quick fixes.

Kimberly's responses help me to know the first day of class that she needs modeling, strategies, and time to dig into challenging texts. Reading fewer works of literature is worth the trade-off if Kimberly learns how to construct meaning with challenging text. Choosing otherwise will leave her ill prepared in college for challenging text, unless, of course, it comes with a SparkNotes version.

There were no SparkNotes in my day. Back then, CliffsNotes was the tool of choice for cheaters. Using CliffsNotes was a hassle. Fortunately, I lived in a metropolitan area and was able to eventually find a bookstore that had the last copy of Cliffs's *Scarlet Letter*. This study "method" was also expensive. I had to spend my own money on gas and the ill-gotten goods. Today, students who wish to avoid reading don't need to go to nearly the trouble or expense that I did. In many cases all they have to do is get online, where for free they can find lots of places to pilfer someone else's constructed meaning. My CliffsNotes has become their online SparkNotes.

Don't get me wrong. SparkNotes.com is a great resource. Unfortunately, some students use this "study aid," without teachers' knowledge, in place of actually doing the reading. These very same readers have no qualms about using the synthesized thinking of Sparks. If a teacher isn't concerned about the personal connections students are making to the texts, and asks them only to retell plot and other details, students who use this method appear to know what they are talking about. They fake their way through tests, quizzes, essays, and discussions. They have learned that it's a great way to play the game of school. Unfortunately, playing this game doesn't help them get smarter when it comes to constructing meaning. Thanks for the heads-up, Kimberly: you remind me of a teenage version of me.

In my days as a high school student, working the system was easy because no one took the time to know me. I could play the game of school with the best of them because no one thought it was their job to know me as a learner. I became skilled in parroting teachers' lectures. I figured out whom to sit next to in case I needed to copy. I became proficient at skimming and scanning the textbook until I found the place that held the same words as the end-of-chapter questions. Because my teachers didn't know me well, cheating was easy most of the time.

I continue reading, and another survey response catches my eye. Grace records what she read last semester in her British Literature class. She writes, "I was assigned to read *Hamlet* and Shakespeare. I liked reading *Hamlet* much better than Shakespeare." No, that isn't a mistake. You read it right. Grace reports that she earned a B despite the fact that she does not remember that Shakespeare actually penned *Hamlet*. I learn from Grace's responses that she doesn't need more British Literature assigned, but rather time to dig into a classic piece and actually be shown different ways to construct meaning when the text is difficult.

Kevin reports that he earned a 92 percent in his last English class and didn't even read. "The teacher wrote dumb questions that were easy to guess the answers to if you listened to the class discussions." Kevin needs to be shown how to construct personal meaning for himself. From his responses, I learn that Kevin thinks that making sense of text is about spitting back answers that are going to be asked on a quiz. He needs to know that reading can make him smarter about the world around him.

Aaron brags, "No reading is hard for me. I am the Mark Twain of reading." I'm not sure what he means by being a "Mark Twain of reading," but he reports that he got a C in his last English class even though he reads "24/7." His responses sound suspicious. One thing for sure, this kid has a sense of humor. I turn over the backside of the survey where I have asked kids to tell me what my competition for their time will be. I want to know if they have a job or are involved in extracurricular activities. Aaron writes, "Well, I am a varsity lacrosse goalie. I don't mess around with that either. I am All-Conference from my junior year, so this year I'm going to work ten times more for my All-State award. Lacrosse is going to take up all of my free time until dark. Then after dark, I will be with my girlfriend. So bottom line, I have no time for homework." His honesty is refreshing, bordering on chilling. Basically Aaron is telling me that I better give him a really good reason to do homework, because if I don't, he's not playing.

Brandon is also honest. On the back of his survey he writes, "Things that get in the way of my homework are work. I work all the time, like 35 hours a week. My girlfriend is a major factor in my life as well. My mom and I live alone so I *gotta* clean up and help around the house. I also have friends who I need to see, and all of them go to high school across town so I have to go there to see them." Brandon is a busy kid. He transferred schools his senior year. I understand that he wants to stay in touch with his buddies. His girlfriend matters, too. She makes sure that he goes to class so he can graduate. Brandon works a lot so he can help his mom pay the bills. This is a reality that more and more kids are facing. Everything that Brandon wrote as competition for his time is important. What he has written helps me remember that my students have very complicated lives outside of school. What bothers me is not what he wrote on the back but what he wrote for the first question, which asks students to list all the texts that are difficult for them to read. Brandon writes, "I really can't read so everything is hard."

Before readers feel too sad for Brandon, let me assure you that he can read. He wouldn't have been able to write the narrative on the back the way he had if he couldn't read. What troubled me about what Brandon wrote was that he didn't think he could read "hard stuff." When it came to academic or challenging text, Brandon quit. He gave up because he didn't think he was smart or strategic enough to do it. The second week of school Brandon dropped my class. I sought him out and begged him to reenroll. He told me he knew that he couldn't think like I was asking the class to think. He had to pass English to graduate, he said emphatically. I promised Brandon that I wouldn't let him fail, that if he came to class and tried, he wouldn't flunk. Sadly, nothing I said could change his mind. Brandon had already given up.

Responses from the Beginning of Course Survey remind me not to assume my students are "getting it." I learn from the surveys early in the year that there are students who struggle when it comes to academic reading and writing. I start to figure out who's good at playing the game of school and who really cares about getting smarter. I find out who the excellent test-takers are and who refuses to play at all. Stretching students to grow as readers and writers requires that I discover who they are as learners. To do this, I have to do more than give them routine tests and quizzes.

Assessment for Students: Using the Data Students Give

I use a slightly different survey for students in reading support classes. The Why Am I in Here? survey is given as close to the first day of school as possible to help me figure out if students know why they have been put in remedial reading (Figure 2.5). Over the years, I've discovered that many

Figure 2.5

Why Am I in Here? Survey

1. Have you ever been in a reading class before? If so, describe what the reading class was like.
2. You did not register for this class. Why do you think it was added to your schedule?
3. What is your attitude about being in another reading class?
4. How well do you think you read compared with other students in your grade?
5. Have you ever seen any of your test scores? If so, what did you learn from the data?

---

struggling readers have unquestioningly accepted their placement in reading support classes. Oddly, their perception of themselves as readers often differs from the courses that have been placed on their schedule. This disconnect doesn't make sense to them, but interestingly enough they accept it. The system has beaten them down, and they have given up control not only of their class schedule but of their learning. I have been surprised by how many of them aren't sure why they are tracked into the classes they are.

The Why Am I in Here? survey gives me not only insight into students' attitudes toward reading, but an entry point to begin discussing who should be in charge of their thinking.

I am always eager to read what students write on this survey. Few struggling readers can explain why their elective was replaced with a remedial reading class. A handful of readers usually admit that they struggle when reading text they don't like. They assume this is why they are in the class. Most have never seen their standardized test scores, and few if any can articulate what their strengths and weaknesses are as readers.

Lela, an African immigrant, has been in the United States for seven years. I get the feeling he is afraid of hurting my feelings as he writes, "I am not disappointed that I am in this class but I am disappointed that I never get to take an elective. I'm just curious about the class I would have had if I wasn't in another reading class."

Adam, on the other hand, couldn't care less about my feelings. He writes, "Yeah, I'm mad I'm in this class. In my opinion, I can read as well as anybody else in here." Given that the room is filled with twenty-four other struggling readers, he's not saying much. I continue reading Adam's response: "I think I can read just fine. The only problem I have is that I don't understand what I read."

Tyler responds to question two with standard interventionist lingo: "I can decode with fluency and accuracy. I only have trouble when it comes to remembering what I've read." It doesn't dawn on Adam or Tyler that not "remembering what they read" is the whole point. Unless they are going to be news anchors, reading fast with expression isn't the main reason people read. I will have to work hard to help them both redefine what it means to be a good reader.

Most students enrolled in Reading Essentials are pretty compliant about their placement. Sadly, they have come to expect it. Danny, a tenth grader, writes that being in another reading class seems "pretty normal." Ricky has "no clue" why he's in reading, and Chaz doesn't care because he's been in one since first grade. Brittany, on the other hand, thinks she reads "just fine." She writes, "I don't read that bad, I just choose not to." Dillon is surprised by his placement because on last year's state test he "put everything he had into it," and Mike reports that he is "irritated" about being in the class.

Kyle writes that he is "indifferent." Red flags go up. *Indifferent* isn't a word typically used by struggling readers on this survey to convey their attitude. I meet with Kyle's counselor and check out his grades from middle school. I discover that he was in all honors classes and earned As and Bs. I examine his schedule for the current year and see that he is in honors English and science. I share with him what I learned and ask him what's going on. He tells me that he "chokes" when it comes to tests. "I'm just not a good test-taker," he says. "I know the information, but when it comes to those bubble-in tests, there aren't any good choices for my thinking."

I'm pretty sure that Kyle's middle school teachers and parents recommended him for the advanced classes, but his summative data indicated his placement in reading. If I don't work hard to challenge Kyle, his time in my class will be wasted. Learning that he is a better student than his test scores indicate is important to know—it will help me differentiate my instruction so he continues to grow. I'm thankful that I've learned this about him the first week.

Jinn, a Korean student, recognizes that he could benefit from a reading class but writes, "I know I need to comprehend better but I don't like being in a class with low kids." Glory jots down, "I read good when I read things I like. When I'm told to read something and I don't like it, I read and my mind wanders." I am struck by Glory's metacognition. She knows she can read well when she likes the material.

Merranda writes, "I think this class will be very nice and relaxing because there will be no homework or pressure." Maybe there is no pressure on her part, but there sure is on mine. One would think that reading six years below one's grade level would mean self-imposed pressure.

The last survey I read is Colin's. Something about what he says strikes a chord inside me. He writes, "I would like to improve my reading so that when I go home, I can read and remember on my own." His desire to be independent aligns perfectly with one of my core teaching beliefs. If reading is going to serve students, they have to be able to use strategies flexibly so they can construct meaning on their own.

If I really want to make a difference in students' learning, I have to show them that ultimately they are the ones in charge of their comprehension. Many students believe that comprehending school reading is out of their control. They have convinced themselves that it is the teacher's job to make them "get it." I have also learned that a lot of students narrowly define the act of reading. They think that if they read the words, meaning will miraculously arrive. When it doesn't, they write it off to just being a bad reader. Having students imitate me using a strategy is one thing. It is a whole new level of competence when they apply a strategy to make meaning for themselves. Helping them become independent learners is my ultimate goal.

When I ask students how they learn, I discover a lot about what they need. Taking advantage of the data I glean from student responses, I begin to jot down some notes. I start brainstorming a "to do" list (Figure 2.6) that will help me begin meeting their needs.

Each year I am astounded by my students' honesty and clarity when it comes to sharing their needs. If I just take the time to ask them what they need, I am handsomely rewarded with a body of information that fills me with empathy and informs my instruction. This data doesn't have a neat row of numbers attached to it, but it gives me a wealth of information that allows me to differentiate for the needs of my students.

Emotional Engagement Drives Cognitive Engagement

The conversation calendars and question surveys are ways for me to tap into my students' emotional engagement. By asking them honest questions that I truly care about, I get to know them deeply. I know how hard I can push, and I know when it's time to back off. When I know about students' lives, they tend to try harder when presented with challenges in the classroom. Perhaps they try harder because they know I care about them as learners. Perhaps it's because they know they have a place to share how they learn best. When I know what their interests are outside of school, I can look for authentic text that helps them see why reading and writing well matters.

This connection allows us both to take risks. I can take the risk of bringing in compelling content while students are more willing to risk

Beginning of the Year "To-Dos"

Create a progress-monitoring folder for each student. Folders will hold summative data, calendars with relevant information, annotated text (one for each quarter), and notes from parents, deans, teachers, and counselors.

Lela

- Give him the course-of-study booklet and let him see all the different electives that are available.
- Set a goal of taking one of those electives second semester. This means I will have to have evidence that he can read beyond his state test scores. Retesting with the Gates-MacGinite in January using a different form is an option. Student work samples are another source of data that I can use to indicate improvement.
- Based on his fall Gates-MacGinite scores, Lela did well on the first two columns of questions. This might mean he got tired and started to guess. Point this out to Lela and suggest that he will need to improve his stamina so he has endurance to read the entire test.
- Find out what is hard for Lela to read. Is he struggling with decoding and fluency, or is his mind wandering when the reading gets boring or difficult?

Brittany

- Brittany is not happy about being in school. Find out why.
- Check out whom she has for English and see if we can work together to help her be successful on the first assignment.
- Find out what Brittany likes to do when she isn't in school. Locate texts that will align with her outside interests.
- Build a need to know for her. Show her how to search on Amazon.com, and point out how she can find books to read that she will like.

Glory

- Point out that recognizing that sometimes she "gets it," and sometimes she doesn't, is something that good readers do. Find out what she already knows how to do when she recognizes confusion.
- Model for her how to ask a question to isolate confusion.

Tyler

- Acknowledge that reading with fluency and accuracy is terrific, but stress that actually remembering and using what you've read is most important.
- Assure him that we will do more than phonic and fluency work in class.
- Show him some examples of annotated text. Point out how readers often annotate as a way to hold thinking and keep their minds from wandering.

Merranda

- Create urgency by sharing with her any recent test data.
- Let Merranda know that time is ticking and that this class isn't about relaxing. It's about becoming a better reader and writer so she will have more access to the world.
- Assure her that the work will be challenging and that I will expect a lot from her. Reassure her that I will be there to support and scaffold her learning when she struggles.

Figure 2.6

new learning. Emotional engagement lets us both know that failure isn't followed by judgment or ridicule. Through talk and text, I build their trust and create a connection that allows me to move them toward deeper cognitive engagement.

When I know my students well, I am a better teacher.

What Works

Assessment Point: Effective assessors know that they have to build time into their workweek to get to know and reflect on who their students are as people. They recognize that they should know their students better than an outsider who hands them a synthesized packet of data. District-delivered data is only a small part of who each student is. It doesn't determine what kind of learner each student can be.

Assessment Point: Effective assessors use what they learn from the data to improve their practice. They know that learners are more willing to take a risk when they know the teacher cares about them as people. They remember that even a small change in an instructional practice can make a huge difference to students.

Assessment Point: Effective assessors know that the way in which students define how they read determines how hard they work at constructing meaning—no matter what content you teach. If they believe that their role is to decode with fluency and your job is to make them get it, you will have to work a lot harder than they do.

"Are You Up for a Challenge?"

1. I learned this first one from Donald Graves's book *The Energy to Teach* (2001). Choose a class that you are struggling with or would like to know better. On a blank sheet of paper, record the name of every student you can remember. Next to each student's name, jot down something that you know about him or her as a learner and/or person. Check your class roster. Whom do you know the best? Who intrigues you? Which student did you forget? Consider how knowing something about each student as an individual might help you connect to him or her in a way that has nothing to do with school. Challenge yourself during the next class period to discover something new about one of your students whom you don't know as well as you could.

2. When school starts, ask your students what they think their role as a reader is. Do they think they should decode with fluency, or do they know that they need

to actively construct meaning? On the last day of school or at the end of the semester, let them reread what they wrote the first day. Encourage them to tell you how their thinking about their role as a reader has changed. This will provide you with progress monitoring data that might come in handy later.

3. Once you learn something about a student, ask him or her to tell you more about it. If you can find a piece of text, such as a newspaper article or poem that relates to something that student cares about, share it with him or her. Notice how your relationship changes with that student. Your student will be honored that you were thinking about him or her outside of class. It could very well give you the patience and energy to do it for others. Before long you will have students willing to follow you into any challenge.

CHAPTER 3

Game-Time Assessment

[Workshop] classrooms are places I want to linger all day because students are . . . reading, writing, talking, laughing, thinking, pausing, figuring, and writing some more . . . The working hum of these classrooms is the sound of happily, intensely engaged learners.

—*Samantha Bennett (2007)*

I t is easier to get to know students deeply and collect meaningful data about them when I'm not standing up in front of my class lecturing the whole time. The workshop model has always kept me honest when it comes to sharing the classroom work with students. As a matter of fact, I've taken the *time* tenet of workshop so seriously that when I plan, my goal is to let students work on their own or in groups for two-thirds of the period, leaving one-third of the time for whole-class instruction. Writing this book, I began to realize that the workshop model was also the key to localizing my assessment practices. Its structure makes it possible for me to assess and immediately begin to address students' needs. When students have the majority of class time to read, write, and discuss, I have the opportunity to gather data that tells me what they need. In this chapter, readers will see how I use the workshop model as a structure for planning instruction and for implementing and using assessment to address student needs.

The Wisdom of Athletic Coaches

It's no secret that I am a sports fan who likes to compare the art of coaching to the art of teaching. Recently, I got a refresher lesson on just how similar the two are.

Toward the end of July, I was asked to present in a small town, smack dab in the middle of serious football country. My plan was to teach the group something about thinking strategies and then let them practice using and integrating the information into their own lesson designs. The plan worked pretty well for most of the teachers. However, there was a group of men in the back who were buying into only part of the game plan.

As long as I was doing the talking, they were polite and seemed engaged. But as soon as I released the whole group to work on using the information to plan for their classes, the men got "off task." They were working on something, but it wasn't strategy instruction, or at least that's what I thought. In an attempt to get these guys back on task, I found myself visiting their part of the room quite often. It was tempting to pull the whole group back together, knowing that I could manage their behavior better if I did. However, I reminded myself that whoever was doing the work was the one getting smarter.

Each time I got closer, their conversation seemed to switch abruptly to reading instruction. As I got within earshot, I could see that their clipboards held white sheets of paper peppered with various configurations of Xs and Os. From the snippets of conversation I did catch, I surmised that my friends in the back were the high school football coaches, and the literacy work they were doing had more to do with football camp than science, social studies, or math. Pretending not to notice, I walked by several more times, catching more bits of the real conversation.

I overheard the defensive coordinator/history teacher say, "Markus hasn't been to the weight room once this summer." There was urgency in his voice, knowing that the August heat was going to hinder players' performance and even be dangerous for kids who weren't in shape.

The guy sitting next to him must have been the conditioning coach/math teacher, because he responded by saying, "Don't worry, coach. I've got a little surprise for the players who didn't work out over the summer. I'll be able to tell in the first five minutes who lifted and who didn't. I've got four different workouts we can hand out, depending on each player's level of conditioning."

I walked away impressed, thinking, *Nice differentiation.*

After lunch, I headed back to the auditorium and found the coaches still in there, eating their lunch and diligently working on their football "stuff." Hoping to find some middle ground with them I asked, "So do you guys have any actual plays you could show me?"

One of the coaches looked up and said, "Can you read them?"

"I'm not sure. I haven't seen too many real playbooks, and I was just curious to see if I could make any sense out of them."

Surprised by my response, the coach with the collection of plays turned his notebook so I could see it. I flipped through the pages, realizing that the plays were pretty involved and that I couldn't make heads or tails of them. Closing the book, I asked, "So, how many players are like me and have trouble reading these?"

"Quite a few at first," answered the defensive coordinator/history teacher. "Usually they are freshmen or new to the game. But by the time these boys are seniors, they know the essentials."

Across the table another coach chimed in, "Yeah, easy for you to say, Herb. You don't coach the offense. I'd like to see you teach James and Walter how to make sense of some of those plays." He looked up at me and said, "It takes forever for some of these kids to understand them well enough so that they can run 'em correctly come game time. Making sense of them in practice is one thing. We expect mistakes. Doing it right when it comes to Friday night is another story."

"May I see the playbook again?" I asked. I randomly picked a page and showed it to him. "How do you read this one?"

The coach began thinking aloud. He pointed out the Xs and Os. Then he drew my attention to the arrows and explained how the play should work, providing everyone did his job. I listened for about thirty seconds to one of the best think-alouds I've ever heard. Curious to know what happens when a play goes wrong, I asked him to show me where players struggle. (See Figure 3.1 for more information about think-alouds.) Again, the offensive coordinator began thinking aloud, sharing what would happen to the quarterback if anyone on the offensive line missed his assignment.

"Assignment?" I asked.

"Didn't do their job," he said. He then told me how the offense reruns the play in practice so that when it counts, the kids know what to do. I thanked him and the other coaches for the insider information and headed to the front of the room. It was time to start the afternoon session. *Thankfully,* I thought, *I had found my middle ground.*

Figure 3.1

How to Do a Think-Aloud

1. Select a piece of text that you want students to be able to read on their own.
2. Read aloud a small chunk of the text.
3. Stop reading and share out loud what you are thinking.
4. Repeat the process.

Practice Strategy

Model, using a piece of text that you actually want students to read. This way you can cover content and show students how to be better readers of it.

Don't do a think-aloud for too long. Make sure you give your students only a taste of how you think. Then release them to practice the thinking themselves.

Don't try to model too much, but be sure to give students multiple opportunities throughout the year to see how you think about text. Consider sharing possible questions, connections, and new ideas you have. Show students how you determine importance or get unstuck. Be as authentic as possible.

Try to remember what it was like for you the first time you read the text. Remind students that meaning doesn't arrive. It has to be constructed. Doing a think-aloud shows students how the best reader in the class thinks when he or she reads.

I kicked off the afternoon session by sharing how much I learn about good instruction from watching successful athletic coaches. I noticed the guys in the back look up from their clipboards. "At lunch," I said, "I was reminded once again how good coaches know to differentiate their coaching and plan their practices so the players get to do the majority of the work.

"Smart coaches model for their players the skills and strategies they want their athletes to master. They plan their practices so the kids have lots of time to rehearse what they are taught. Coaches know that it's not effective or efficient to 'grade' everything their athletes do in practice. Instead they give real-time feedback so players can keep getting better. They work together to be the best they can be. In fact, the best coaches run an almost perfect workshop when it comes to game-time preparation. Games serve as the tests."

During the afternoon break, I ran into one of the coaches at the soda machine. He said, "I liked it when you compared the workshop model to coaching. It makes me think that if I can do it on the field, I should be able to do it in the classroom."

"Sure you can," I said. "What you do on the field for kids to make them better athletes is the same thing you need to do for them in the classroom to make them more successful learners. Coach them how to read your content the way you read it. While they are practicing what you've shown them, circulate and give them feedback and support. You may have to model again just like you do for the athletes who don't run the play correctly the first time. Before students leave for their next class, bring them together like you do your offensive line, and help them synthesize the big ideas. If you can do it for football players, you can do it for students."

"Thanks," he said, and walked away with a smile.

Practice Time for the Game of Life

Just like the athletes on the field who do the majority of the work during practice, students in my classroom do the majority of the work by reading, writing, and thinking during class. By organizing my time using the workshop model (Figure 3.2) every day, all year long, I can ensure that their reading, writing, and thinking are getting better.

In its simplest form, the workshop model has four basic parts: opening, mini-lesson, work time, and debriefing.

- The **opening** is an opportunity to share the day's learning targets and set the stage for the day.
- During the **mini-lesson** the teacher provides direct instruction for the whole class.
- During the **work time**, students get to dig in and practice the learning. This is the most important part of the workshop and therefore must be the longest part of the period. I try to give students the bulk of the class period to work, practice, or apply what has been taught during the mini-lesson.
  - ¤ As students work, I confer with individuals or small groups. Often my conferences are pretty short—about two to four minutes long. The purpose of conferring is twofold. I want to assess student learning and help them to build stamina. When I confer, I try to figure out what students know and what they need so they can continue doing the work on their own. My goal when conferring isn't to "fix" students but rather to provide support and scaffolding so students can be the ones who engage in the critical thinking. Just like during the mini-lesson, I must be careful not to take time away from students' doing the work. Conferring helps me help students stay on task so they can build stamina, skill, and endurance. For more on conferring, see Chapter 6.

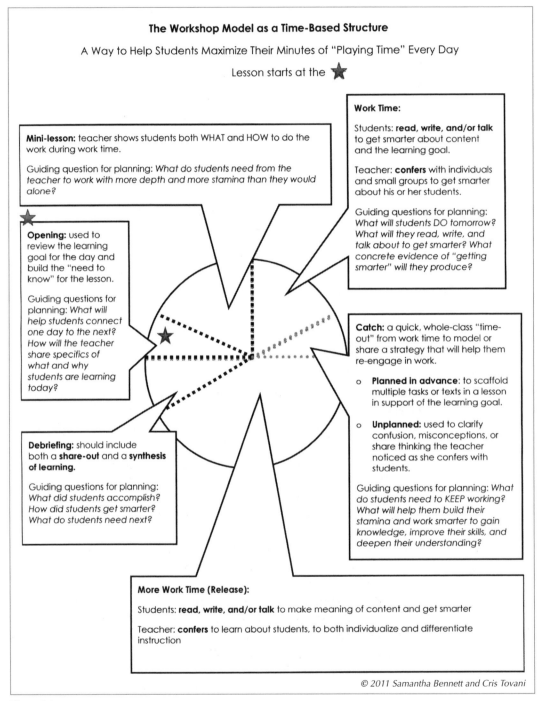

The Workshop Model as a Time-Based Structure

A Way to Help Students Maximize Their Minutes of "Playing Time" Every Day

Lesson starts at the ⭐

Work Time:

Students: **read, write, and/or talk** to get smarter about content and the learning goal.

Teacher: **confers** with individuals and small groups to get smarter about his or her students.

Guiding questions for planning: *What will students DO tomorrow? What will they read, write, and talk about to get smarter? What concrete evidence of "getting smarter" will they produce?*

Mini-lesson: teacher shows students both WHAT and HOW to do the work during work time.

Guiding question for planning: *What do students need from the teacher to work with more depth and more stamina than they would alone?*

Opening: used to review the learning goal for the day and build the "need to know" for the lesson.

Guiding questions for planning: *What will help students connect one day to the next? How will the teacher share specifics of what and why students are learning today?*

Catch: a quick, whole-class "time-out" from work time to model or share a strategy that will help them re-engage in work.

o   **Planned in advance**: to scaffold multiple tasks or texts in a lesson in support of the learning goal.

o   **Unplanned:** used to clarify confusion, misconceptions, or share thinking the teacher noticed as she confers with students.

Guiding questions for planning: *What do students need to KEEP working? What will help them build their stamina and work smarter to gain knowledge, improve their skills, and deepen their understanding?*

Debriefing: should include both a **share-out** and a **synthesis of learning.**

Guiding questions for planning: *What did students accomplish? How did students get smarter? What do students need next?*

More Work Time (Release):

Students: **read, write, and/or talk** to make meaning of content and get smarter

Teacher: **confers** to learn about students, to both individualize and differentiate instruction

© 2011 Samantha Bennett and Cris Tovani

Figure 3.2

◻ Catch-and-release occurs during the work time and can be either a planned or an unplanned part of the workshop. In her book *That Workshop Book: New Systems and Structures for Classrooms That Read, Write, and Think* (2007), Samantha Bennett describes how her colleague Peter Thulson refers to a "catch-and-release" model of workshop. When I use the catch-and-release technique, it is because I have noticed a pattern of confusion in several students. Instead of repeating the teaching to each individual student, I temporarily halt the work time to quickly share a strategy or a piece of content that will benefit the class's learning process. Other times when I use catch-and-release, I've anticipated places where students might struggle. In these cases, I model a way to negotiate the difficulty and then I release the kids so they have time to practice what I showed them. In either case, the catches are short, usually lasting only a few minutes.

• The **debriefing** occurs at the end of the workshop and gives students an opportunity to be metacognitive as they synthesize, reflect on, and name what they have learned for the day.

Whether learners are struggling, gifted, or in between, they all deserve a year's worth of growth. When they get two-thirds of each class period to work, the minutes of practice time add up. When there is intentional planning with student work minutes in mind, combined with a teacher by their side conferring and giving targeted feedback, students can't help but expand their knowledge and increase their skills. This means they can tackle any kind of text with confidence and have the wherewithal to know what they need to do to construct meaning. If we do our jobs well, by listening to teach instead of talking to teach, students should be just as exhausted as teachers at the end of the day—and just as brilliant.

The Workshop Model Then and Now

Readers familiar with the workshop model aren't surprised that athletes and artisans alike embrace its fundamental components. In the early 1980s, pioneers such as Lucy Calkins, Donald Graves, and Nancie Atwell gave educators their first taste of what the workshop model looks like in a classroom setting. From these experts, teachers learned that there were essential components that had to be in place so students could have more control of their learning: time, ownership, and response. Students need a large chunk of **time** to read, write, and discuss their learning. They need **ownership** through choice in what they read and write. And they need opportunities to give their **response** and to get a response from others.

When it was first introduced, the workshop model found its foothold at the elementary level. Thanks to Atwell's groundbreaking book, *In the Middle* (1998), it also became a mainstay of many middle school language arts classrooms. Sadly, not enough high school teachers embraced the structure as a viable option for instruction.

As an elementary teacher, I found that planning with the components of the workshop model worked for me, so when I moved to high school, it made sense to structure my two remedial reading classes using the same model. For years, the course was even titled Readers Workshop. I didn't, however, use the same planning structure when it came to my three other English classes. The reason? It was unmanageable for me to match seventy-five different students to their "just right" level books and cover the required course content.

At the secondary level, students who struggle to read and write well are expected to master the same content as their more skilled reading and writing peers. In a perfect world, or at least in a world where the teacher has only twenty-five to thirty students, adhering to the original components of the workshop model is manageable. However, in multiple classrooms full of skeptical, struggling adolescent readers and writers, I realized that the original components had to be slightly tweaked.

Addressing a Cornerstone of Workshop: Choice

As learners progress through the grade levels, the urgency for them to master content becomes more pronounced. Believing that students need time, ownership, and response, I stubbornly refused to abandon these components for content coverage. Instead, I decided to see how I could meld the components of workshop with the realities of secondary classrooms.

My first challenge was making sure that students retained ownership of their learning. This meant I had to build choice into my classroom as much as possible. I quickly discovered that I couldn't monitor five sections of students all reading different books. It was too easy for students to fake read, and because they were choosing only certain things to read, I couldn't have fidelity to the curriculum. However, I just couldn't give up the choice piece. Students needed at least some say in what they read, how they responded, and how they showed their understanding. So here is my compromise, a combination of the following:

- whole-class anchor texts supported by nonfiction choices (six to eight weeks);
- an ongoing, concurrent, choice-based reading structure; and

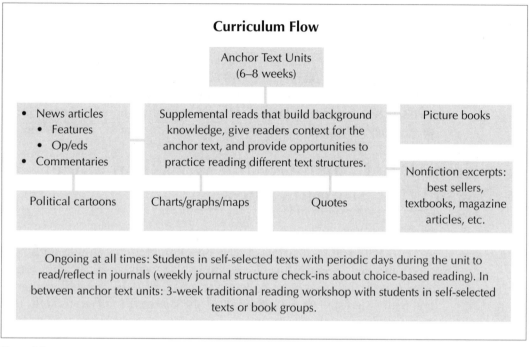

Curriculum Flow

Anchor Text Units
(6–8 weeks)

- News articles
  - Features
  - Op/eds
- Commentaries

Supplemental reads that build background knowledge, give readers context for the anchor text, and provide opportunities to practice reading different text structures.

Picture books

Political cartoons

Charts/graphs/maps

Quotes

Nonfiction excerpts: best sellers, textbooks, magazine articles, etc.

Ongoing at all times: Students in self-selected texts with periodic days during the unit to read/reflect in journals (weekly journal structure check-ins about choice-based reading). In between anchor text units: 3-week traditional reading workshop with students in self-selected texts or book groups.

Figure 3.3

- shorter (three-week) units in which students read self-selected texts in class or join book clubs to read with peers. (See Figure 3.3.)

Initially I start a unit of study with a whole-class read that I refer to as an *anchor text*. I use this whole-class read to demonstrate different reading and writing strategies that I want students to use. I also use the anchor text to teach content required by the school/district/state. While we are using the anchor text, I give students choice in their reading by providing several supplemental pieces that are intended to build background knowledge, give readers context for the unit of study, and provide them with opportunities to practice reading different text structures. Usually the supplemental text choices are short, high interest, and accessible.

When the class has finished the anchor text, I like to move students into book clubs where I manage their choice by providing three to five titles around the unit's guiding questions. Students choose their book based on interest and reading level. Some teachers may worry that their students will choose books that are too easy. Of course this is something to consider, but when it happens, it's my job to find more intriguing titles that will encourage students to read outside their comfort level.

Choice is very important to me, and although students are required to have an ongoing self-selected book, I also provide time for them to do free reading in class. At least once a quarter, students have a three-week opportunity to read anything they choose. During these three-week periods, they use their self-selected books to examine author's craft, study conventions of language, or increase fluency, vocabulary, stamina, and comprehension.

Throughout this chapter, you will notice that I have tried to remain true to the essential components of workshop. Perhaps you will recognize your own struggles in mine and notice different ways that I have tried to reconcile the realities of secondary instruction with the components of workshop.

Be a Game-Day Coach: Use the Workshop Model to Assess What Students Know

Years ago, I visited a biology teacher's classroom. She was lecturing on cell structures. It was fascinating to hear how complex these building blocks are. I listened intently for fifty minutes and walked away with a new appreciation for the human body. I was amazed by the teacher's expertise and truly interested in the information she shared. I noticed, though, that many students in the classroom had their heads down or had work from other classes on their desks. Even though I was enthralled, I was curious to know what the kids walked away with. So after thanking the teacher for letting me sit in on her lecture, I said, "I learned so much today. What do you think your students learned?"

The teacher looked at me kind of funny and said, "Oh, I won't know that until the chapter test."

"When's the chapter test?" I asked.

"In a couple of weeks," she said.

I thought to myself, *A couple of weeks? Seriously? What if half the class fails, then what? In a couple of weeks it will be too late for the kids who checked out today. They will be lost. As the information in the science class gets more complicated, they will get further behind.* This got my wheels spinning and took me back to the wisdom of great coaches.

Some coaches are universally feared by their opponents. Rivals speak of them as great "game-day" coaches. Mention the names Vince Lombardi or John Wooden, and sports fanatics get an immediate vision of a coach who helps his team rise to any challenge and pull off miraculous victories, again and again. These coaches are revered for their ability to regroup and adjust *during the game* to ensure victory at the end.

If they want to win, game-day coaches don't wait until Monday morning to look at statistics. They know that by then it is too late to win the game. At halftime, they quickly scour first-half game films, looking for weaknesses in their adversaries that they can exploit. They pay attention to plays that are working, and figure out how to implement them more in the second half. They aren't afraid to analyze stats because they know it may help them discover a pattern that will inform their third-quarter play selection. This type of formative assessment provides "real-time" information that allows adjustments to be made quickly.

Just like coaches, teachers need a way to figure out what kids know and need on a "real-time" basis. They need ways to alter lesson plans so that they can adjust their instruction to meet learners' individual needs, right now. Planning with the workshop model in mind allows me to assess all period, not just at the end of the unit.

What Works

Assessment Point: Effective assessors know that they aren't being lazy when they stop talking so students can do the work. They take advantage of student work time to assess, differentiate, and give meaningful feedback. They recognize that meaning doesn't arrive but requires time to be constructed. Like successful athletes, students need time to practice. Great athletes don't become great by listening. They achieve their goals because they are the ones doing the work. Effective assessors let their students DO.

"Are You Up for a Challenge?"

Coaches know that the more their athletes practice, the better they will be when it is time to perform. The same is true for students. Consider the amount of instructional time you have with them. Instead of planning what you will do during that time, plan what you want students to do. Set a goal to shift some of the minutes you normally use talking to the students to work time so they can practice what you've taught.

As an initial goal, work toward splitting the class time fifty/fifty with your students. If you get half the time to talk, give them the other half to do the work. Remember, you still get to teach, but while students are working, you are conferring, giving feedback, and planning in your head what kids will need tomorrow. Make it your *ultimate time-sharing goal* to talk only one-third of the period and give the other two-thirds to students to do the work.

As you plan, ask yourself, "How will students work tomorrow? What will they read? What will they write? What will they talk about?" Anticipate where learners might stumble and need scaffolding. Know that the longer they work with your guidance and feedback, the more deeply they will understand the material.

CHAPTER 4

Off the Field and Into the Classroom

When teachers join forces with their students in the formative assessment process, their partnership generates powerful learning outcomes. Teachers become more effective, students become actively engaged, and they both become intentional learners.

—*Connie Moss and Susan Brookhart (2009)*

To help readers envision how the workshop model can maximize student work time and provide a way to immediately assess student learning, I have included scripts of actual workshops with my students. Readers will notice how I use workshop time to plan and to give students feedback that will help them grow every day as readers, writers, and thinkers. Below is an excerpt from a unit of study about illegal immigration. *Crossing the Wire* by Will Hobbs is the anchor text, but embedded in each class period are supplemental texts that students can choose from to deepen their understanding of the complexities of immigration. I use the tenets of backward design explained by Wiggins and McTighe in their work, *Understanding by Design* (2005) to plan my units. Chapters 6 and 7 describe this aspect of planning in more depth.

The following example is a real-time description of one ninety-minute block from my ninth-grade English class. While you read, notice how each part of the lesson helps me

1. maximize time for students to do the work;
2. assess, instruct, and differentiate for individual needs to ensure maximum learning for each student.

Day One Workshop Focus: Making Thinking Visible Using *Crossing the Wire* by Will Hobbs

As students walk in, they see the following learning target chart written on the whiteboard. (For more on learning targets, see Chapter 7.)

Learning Targets	Assessments
I can show how I am thinking about text in a variety of ways.	inner-voice sheets
Instead of saying, "I don't get it," I can ask a question that might help me build background knowledge to answer my question.	sticky notes

In an attempt to let students in on the assessment process, I identify each day what I want them to know and be able to do by the end of the period. On the chart above, the left-hand side identifies daily learning targets. Essentially they are our learning goals for the day. Sometimes the goal is the same for an entire week, depending on how complex the target is. At the end of the period, I need to be able to see how students are progressing. Therefore, on the right-hand side of the chart above, I have identified the formative assessments students will create to show what they have learned. When students know what I want them to learn and how they are going to show me their understanding, our time together is more productive.

(The times listed below are approximations, identified so readers can gauge how long I spend on each section of the workshop.)

7:20–7:30 Opening Structure

As kids trickle in, I greet them and point them to the materials they'll need for the day. "Hi, guys. Grab your calendars, novels, and journals, and make sure you look at the learning targets on the board before we get started. Who can tell me how they think we'll spend our time today, based on the learning targets?"

Cindy raises her hand. "It looks like we're going to read some more and do more of our inner-voice sheets."

"You've got it. But we aren't just going to continue reading the way we did last class. We are going to try to read *differently* today—I want you to read even 'smarter' than you did on Monday. We're going to do that by focusing on questions we care about. They will drive our reading and help us understand the story better. Let's get started."

7:30–7:45 Mini-Lesson

Good readers know there are lots of ways to think and respond to text.

When I read students' inner-voice sheets from the day before, I noticed a pattern. Many students responded only superficially to the novel. They didn't show their thinking in a variety of ways. From their work, I noticed students paraphrased parts they read or asked questions about unknown words. This is a good start, but they need to go deeper, beyond plot, to make personal meaning. I want students to begin to predict, infer, and connect new information to their existing background knowledge. The topic for today's mini-lesson emerged from looking at their work from the previous day.

I make a copy of Omar's inner-voice sheet and with his permission, put it on the document camera so the whole class can read it (see Figure 4.1). To begin the mini-lesson, I share a couple of the inner-voice boxes aloud so the students can see the different ways Omar responded. "Okay, you guys, look up here. Omar did something good readers do. Omar asked a question that helps him clarify something in the story he is not sure of. See where he writes, 'How many days are they on [in the desert] because a human can't go for three weeks without water before they die.' Notice that he is not just retelling the story or asking questions he doesn't care about."

After labeling other things Omar did well, we create an anchor chart of possible ways to respond to reading and hang the chart at the front of the room for students to refer to if they get stuck. (See Figure 4.2; for more information on annotating, see Chapter 5.) By showing examples of student work during the mini-lesson, I give students another model, beyond me, of what thinking can look like. While I share what Omar wrote, I can also fill in some gaps about the plot for readers who missed something from their reading the night before.

After creating our anchor chart, I look at the clock and set our work time goal. I say to the kids, "Last time we read and worked on our inner-voice

Figure 4.1
Omar's Inner-
Voice Sheet

Name *Omar*
Period *1 Blue*
Date *9/28*

INNER-VOICE SHEET

Title of Book __Crossing the Wire__

Author of Book __Will Hobbs__

Directions: Begin reading on page __86__. Record the conversation you have in your head as you read. Be sure to have **at least four (4) sentences per box**. If you catch yourself using a reading strategy, add that at the bottom of the box. Also decide if the conversation inside your head distracts you from making meaning or if the voice helps you interact with the text.

Inner Voice on page 86-89	Inner Voice on page 90-93
• Why is Miguel all beaten up with bruised eye, and stiches, and no teeths? ?Great question! Vigilantes beat him up. Do you remember that word? • If I was victor I would tell migeul to not go with the coyotes. • So the pollos are carying coyotes Drugs and are called Drug runners. Yes or mules.	• So when the coyotes left the group where Miguel was who crossed them? I don't know. Should we figure this out together or have you already done it? • Miguel is explaning How the Migra catch them but are not bad. Migra won't be as bad as the drug runners or Mexican police. • How many days are they on because a human can't go for three weeks out of water before they die. True
Inner Voice on page 96 - 100	Inner Voice on page ___

Figure 4.2

When We Annotate, What Can We Write?

Record a REACTION to something that strikes us.

Ask a QUESTION about something that has happened in the novel.

Give an OPINION on how we might respond in a similar situation.

Make a CONNECTION to the information we read and to what we know.

PREDICT what we think might happen next.

sheets for twenty-five minutes. Today, let's see if we can go thirty-five." Students then have a few minutes to gather their books, inner-voice sheets, and writing utensils before they settle in. Within minutes, they are reading and writing while I survey the room to see who needs my attention.

7:45–8:35 Work Time

I know from the inner-voice sheets I checked the night before that three kids need my attention right away. Isra is brand new, and she isn't sure what is going on in the book or in class. I grab my annotated copy of *Crossing the Wire* and meet with her first. Quickly, I summarize the plot for the first ninety-two pages, which most of the class has already read. I model how to do the inner-voice sheet, and then I let her choose if she wants to begin on page 93 or start at the beginning. She decides to start at the beginning.

Next, I head over to Raymond. He has written only three sentences on his inner-voice sheet. I'm not sure if he doesn't understand how to do the sheet or if the book is too hard for him. After a quick conference, I figure out I'm wrong on both counts. Raymond tells me that he really likes the book and doesn't want to stop and write. I have him read aloud the next page to see if he can decode and summarize it for me. He can, so I explain that if he doesn't show me his thinking, I won't know how to help him. We compromise. He agrees that during the last five minutes of work time he will record something that strikes him about the day's reading and any questions that he has on the inner-voice sheet. He also agrees to record any unfamiliar words that he comes across so that he can add them to his vocabulary notebook.

I zigzag across the room for a quick check-in with Andrea. She is an athlete and has fallen behind in the reading because of her grueling practice and game schedule. She has brought her book to class today and tells me she read for an hour the night before. To check her comprehension, I have her tell me what she remembers from the previous night's reading. When I am satisfied that she has understood what she has read, I praise her for working so hard to catch up, and head over to Hermon.

I notice that Hermon and Vanessa are chatting quietly. As I approach, they both look down at their books and pretend to read. I kneel down so that I am just below their eye level. Positioning myself this way puts students at ease. I think it gives them a feeling of control when I'm not looming over them, demanding a correct response. "How's it going?" I ask.

"Terrible," Hermon says. "This book is so boring."

"Hmm. I wonder if you got stuck somewhere in the last twenty pages, because you're the first one to complain that this book is boring. What's the last part you remember?"

Hermon takes me back to page 78. "I'm behind," she says with a sheepish look.

"Okay, well, let's get caught up. I think I can help you, but I need to know what you last remember reading."

Hermon starts to recount plot, and I can quickly tell that she is confused by Julio, a character who has returned to the plotline. She doesn't understand how he is going to cross the border by using inner tubes to float down the flood channels. I try to help Hermon picture in her head what is happening in the story. I look to my right and see that Vanessa is listening intently. I make eye contact with her and ask, "Vanessa, did you get that part?"

Vanessa says, "Sort of, but I'm not sure why it is so dangerous. I think Victor should go with Julio."

Confusion about the novel is what pulled Vanessa and Hermon off track. I realize that they need some "just-in-time" instruction. I quickly explain the danger of riding an inner tube through a flood channel and share that the main character is afraid of drowning. I then read a couple of pages quietly out loud. After reading two pages, I turn to the girls and ask, "Do you think you can keep going?" Both agree that they are ready to read. Together we set a goal of the number of pages they will read for homework. I encourage them to record any questions they have on their inner-voice sheets so that I can help them the next day if they get stuck. They nod, signaling that they are ready to dig back into the work. "Way to stick with it," I say. They smile. It's time for me to move on.

I survey the room. It seems everyone is reading and on track. I move through the desks, peeking over students' shoulders so I can read what they have written on their inner-voice sheets. When I can clear up confusion with a bit of information, I quietly lean over and share what I know with the student. Trying not to waste one minute of time, I take advantage of the opportunity to do a little grading. Sometimes I read a box on the inner-voice sheet and write "+5" next to it, or underline in pen a sentence I want to remember. The five points that I assign students tells me the box is complete and graded. Underlining specific lines that students have written tells them that their thinking should be shared with the class during the debriefing.

Sometimes I put a star in the right-hand corner to signal that this paper has thinking on it that I might want to share in a mini-lesson the next day. I also jot down brief notes in my conferring notebook. The notations I write serve as evidence that will help me determine individual growth. It is important for me to record what I learn about each student, because it will be an invaluable tool for progress monitoring. The following is an example of a few of my conferring notebook entries (Figure 4.3):

Figure 4.3

Conferring Notes

9/28 Conferences

Perla: Finished *Crossing the Wire*. Invited her to pick another book to read from the Immigration text set. She chose *Into the Beautiful North*. This book might be too hard. Check in with her on Wednesday.

Nichelle: Page 92. She says, "I answered my own question." She was so excited that the question she asked on her inner-voice sheet got answered today.

Vanessa and Hermon: Off task because of confusion. Weren't sure how to reenter the text. Set a goal to read to page 110 by Friday.

Brizhay: Page 98. She says, "I think because Miguel is hurt, he will get caught." Brizhay made predictions today that were logical and followed the plot of the story.

Marcus: Page 97. Doesn't have his glasses, which makes close-up work difficult. The frames are broken and he doesn't want to tell his dad. Excited that he read 25 pages on his own last night. Brainstormed ideas for getting the glasses fixed.

As readers can see in Figure 4.3, my conferring notes are short. I don't have a lot of time to write, so my goal is to record the student's name, date, and what page he or she is on. I jot down one piece of information I've learned about the student as a reader or writer, and I try to give that student a task or information that will nudge him or her along.

From my conferring notes, I have a record of growth that helps me document a year's worth of learning for each student. When I look at the notes I've written or the work I've collected over time from students, I can set individual reading, writing, and thinking goals that will help them master the content.

8:35–8:50 Debriefing

Today, we have only about fifteen minutes to complete the debriefing of the workshop. Instead of sharing in a big group, I ask the kids to get with a partner and share one box from their inner-voice sheet. I ask them to help each other get smarter by clearing up a confusing part or sharing something they figured out. As students talk, I circulate around the room, assessing what I hear. Once again I look for patterns—what they understand and where they are confused. Careful attention to this part of the workshop helps me target my next mini-lesson and lets students know they will be held accountable for the work time every day.

Before students leave, I ask for an exit ticket. I have students record on a sticky note one question they have about the book. As they head out the door, I collect the notes and their inner-voice sheets. I will use these documents as formative assessments to decide what instruction kids will need in the next class.

Workshop as a Structure for Assessment

Besides increasing students' "practice time," the workshop model provides an opportunity to observe learners in action. Teachers have a chance during the work time to clear up confusion and help students deepen their knowledge. They also have the opportunity to collect evidence of student thinking—such as sticky notes and inner-voice sheets—that serves as data. The thinking or data that students leave informs how I will make my instructional adjustments.

In the book *Classroom Assessment for Student Learning: Doing It Right, Using It Well* (2004), Rick Stiggins et al. offer seven strategies for assessing learning that I have begun to layer into my daily workshop (Figure 4.4). When I plan my instruction, I try to keep these questions in mind. Based on her work in my classroom, my instructional coach, Sam Bennett, pointed out how I use these formative assessment practices within the workshop template. Each segment of the workshop gives teachers an opportunity to assess student thinking and address what students need to master content. Implementing this model helps teachers, like coaches, use assessment to enhance performance (Figure 4.5).

Figure 4.4

Stiggins's Seven Practices of Assessment FOR Learning

Where am I going?

- Provide a clear and understandable vision of the learning target.
- Use examples and models of strong and weak work.

Where am I now?

- Offer regular descriptive feedback.
- Teach students to self-assess and set goals.

How can I close the gap?

- Design lessons to focus on one aspect of quality at a time.
- Teach students focused revision.
- Engage students in self-reflection, and let them keep track of and share their learning.

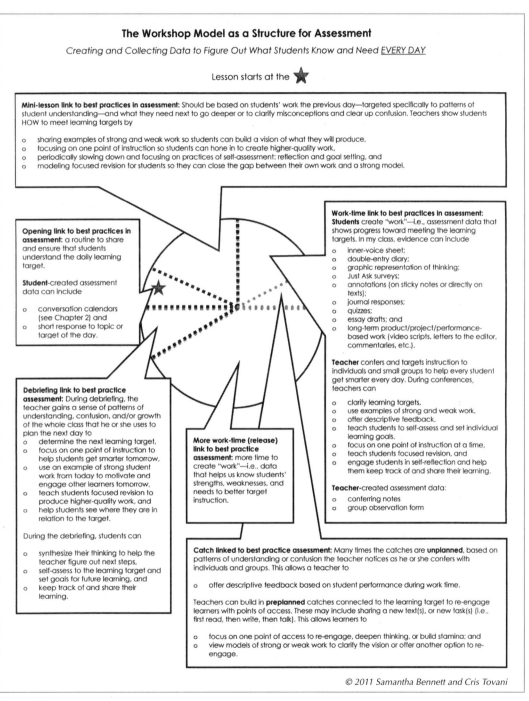

The Workshop Model as a Structure for Assessment

Creating and Collecting Data to Figure Out What Students Know and Need UNDERLINE EVERY DAY

Lesson starts at the ★

Mini-lesson link to best practices in assessment: Should be based on students' work the previous day—targeted specifically to patterns of student understanding—and what they need next to go deeper or to clarify misconceptions and clear up confusion. Teachers show students HOW to meet learning targets by

- o sharing examples of strong and weak work so students can build a vision of what they will produce,
- o focusing on one point of instruction so students can hone in to create higher-quality work,
- o periodically slowing down and focusing on practices of self-assessment: reflection and goal setting, and
- o modeling focused revision for students so they can close the gap between their own work and a strong model.

Opening link to best practices in assessment: a routine to share and ensure that students understand the daily learning target.

Student-created assessment data can include

- o conversation calendars (see Chapter 2) and
- o short response to topic or target of the day.

Work-time link to best practices in assessment: **Students** create "work"—i.e., assessment data that shows progress toward meeting the learning targets. In my class, evidence can include

- o inner-voice sheet;
- o double-entry diary;
- o graphic representation of thinking;
- o Just Ask surveys;
- o annotations (on sticky notes or directly on texts);
- o journal responses;
- o quizzes;
- o essay drafts; and
- o long-term product/project/performance-based work (video scripts, letters to the editor, commentaries, etc.).

Teacher confers and targets instruction to individuals and small groups to help every student get smarter every day. During conferences, teachers can

- o clarify learning targets,
- o use examples of strong and weak work,
- o offer descriptive feedback,
- o teach students to self-assess and set individual learning goals,
- o focus on one point of instruction at a time,
- o teach students focused revision, and
- o engage students in self-reflection and help them keep track of and share their learning.

Teacher-created assessment data:

- o conferring notes
- o group observation form

Debriefing link to best practice assessment: During debriefing, the teacher gains a sense of patterns of understanding, confusion, and/or growth of the whole class that he or she uses to plan the next day to
- o determine the next learning target,
- o focus on one point of instruction to help students get smarter tomorrow,
- o use an example of strong student work from today to motivate and engage other learners tomorrow,
- o teach students focused revision to produce higher-quality work, and
- o help students see where they are in relation to the target.

During the debriefing, students can

- o synthesize their thinking to help the teacher figure out next steps,
- o self-assess to the learning target and set goals for future learning, and
- o keep track of and share their learning.

More work-time (release) link to best practice assessment: more time to create "work"—i.e., data that helps us know students' strengths, weaknesses, and needs to better target instruction.

Catch linked to best practice assessment: Many times the catches are **unplanned**, based on patterns of understanding or confusion the teacher notices as he or she confers with individuals and groups. This allows a teacher to

- o offer descriptive feedback based on student performance during work time.

Teachers can build in **preplanned** catches connected to the learning target to re-engage learners with points of access. These may include sharing a new text(s), or new task(s) (i.e., first read, then write, then talk). This allows learners to

- o focus on one point of access to re-engage, deepen thinking, or build stamina; and
- o view models of strong or weak work to clarify the vision or offer another option to re-engage.

Figure 4.5

Planning with Students' Needs in Mind: Time to Differentiate

From the chart (Figure 4.5), readers will notice that the big chunk of time in the middle of the workshop is a perfect opportunity to differentiate instruction. During the work time students practice, create, and produce thinking. While they work, I can teach small groups, assess what students have written, confer with individuals, and figure out what the class—as a whole—needs next. I use what I observe during work time to plan in my head possible mini-lessons for the next day. Better yet, I can do "just in time instruction" by modeling a thinking process or reteaching a concept. I can also assign points to work that a student and I have discussed during a conference. If I notice that only a few students are struggling with a process or a piece of content, I call that small group of students together to give them more instructional support rather than planning a mini-lesson for the whole class. When I don't pay attention to what students are doing during work time, I end up planning in a vacuum and not giving them what they need.

The evidence that I collect isn't very fancy. Sometimes I collect a sticky note during the debriefing where students have written one thing they understand and one question they still have. (See Figure 4.6 for more debriefing ideas.) Another option is to collect pieces of text that students annotated during the work time. Sometimes my evidence is just a short comment written in my conferring notebook. The data is simple but powerful, in that it helps me to know each student as a learner. Paying careful attention to what kids do during the work time is crucial, because it drives the other three components of the workshop. Each day the learning targets (which I share during the opening structure) and the mini-lesson are based on students' progress or lack of progress from the previous day.

The evidence of thinking that students leave behind helps me think about individual needs as I plan. If I want Perla to continue reading and building background knowledge about illegal immigration, I need to make sure she has another piece of text to read once she finishes the anchor text. If I want Marcus to read an article about immigration, he will need a piece of text that has been enlarged, because his glasses are broken. Differentiation is about adjusting my instruction to meet more student needs. It isn't about each student doing an elaborate, individualized project. I can't manage that with a class of thirty, let alone five sections of thirty students.

Figure 4.6

Debriefings Are Crucial to Student Learning

Regular opportunities to debrief not only hold students accountable for the way they use their work time, but also give teachers a second chance to assess what students need next. Allowing students to be metacognitive at the end of the period and share new learning makes others in the class smarter, and it gives the teacher insight into students' patterns of understanding and confusion.

Options for Debriefing:

- Create a class anchor chart that synthesizes thinking that students will need to go back to over time.
- Ask students to "turn and talk" to articulate their thinking. Next, have them write in their journals to solidify new thinking. Or reverse the order: write to synthesize, and then talk to articulate.
- Allow students time to reflect on the learning target by writing in their response journals.
- Have students write a lingering question on a sticky note to help you figure out the direction for the next day.
- Have students share orally how their thinking has changed since the beginning of class. How are they smarter now than they were ninety minutes ago?
- Have students share what they created during work time with a partner or a group. This allows students to see multiple models of a product and can help them build a vision of high-quality work.

During work time, attention to differentiation might require that I do the following:

- Locate different levels of text on the same topic so students can continue improving their reading skills but also build more background knowledge.
- Adjust assignments so students who are more advanced aren't held back while struggling readers can still work to construct meaning without feeling like they have to "fake it" or cheat to survive.
- Provide more modeling to students who need it.
- Let students who are better readers read ahead.
- Provide alternative ways for struggling readers to access rich text when reading on their own isn't possible. This may mean loading the book onto a listening device or summarizing sections of the plot so the student who struggles can still participate in class and small-group discussions.
- Assign different ways for students to demonstrate understanding.

When it comes to using the workshop model as a structure for assessment, I can collect several pieces of evidence during the work time that serve as data for tomorrow's instruction. These formative assessments help me to know how to better differentiate for individual needs. I can use what I collect to plan for whole-class mini-lessons and individual conferences. Best of all, I can do "just in time" teaching so that kids can dig back into their work.

For example, at the end of the previous workshop, I asked the class to write one question they had about *Crossing the Wire* on a sticky note. After reading the inner-voice sheets and the sticky notes they left with me, I can tell that students need more background knowledge on the issue of illegal immigration. So I get online and type "Colorado/Arizona/Texas illegal immigration" into a search engine.

I select five articles that represent a variety of related topics and reading levels (see Figure 4.7). Recognizing that choice drives engagement, I make ten copies of each article so that students can choose one to read. Their

Figure 4.7

Supplementary Articles for Immigration Study

Alonso, Oswald, and Katherine Corcoran. 2010. "14-Year-Old: Mexican Drug Gang Made Me Behead 4." *Denverpost.com*, December 3.

Alonzo, Monica. 2010. "Seized! Inside the Brutal World of American's Kidnapping Capital: Phoenix, Arizona." *Westword*, August 12–18.

Flores, Aileen B. 2010. "Separated from Family." *El Paso Times*, September 12.

Gergen, David. 2010. "A Smart Exception." *Parade*, June 13.

Glick, Daniel. 2010. "Illegal, but American." *Denver Post,* August 20.

Latimer, Clay. 2010. "Do Immigrants Reduce Crime?" *Coloradoan*, September.

McCombs, Brady. 2010. "July Proved Deadly Month for Migrants." *Arizona Daily Star*, August 3.

Navarrette, Ruben, Jr. 2010. "Politics Interrupts Youthful Dreams." *Denverpost.com*, August 29.

Vaughan, Kevin. 2010. "Mexican Cop Slain; Probed Lake Case." *Denver Post,* October 13.

Vedantam, Shankar. 2010. "ICE Set to Let More Go Free." *Washington Post,* August 28.

Whaley, Monte. 2007. "Swift Raid Effects Still Felt." *Denverpost.com*, November 1.

Wilkinson, Tracy. 2010. "Mexican Drug Trafficker Blamed in Killing of Second Mayor." *Los Angeles Times*, August 30.

Zakin, Susan. 2000. "The Hunters and the Hunted: The Arizona-Mexico Border Turns Into the 21st Century Frontier." *High Country News*, October 9.

choice will depend on the question they asked the previous day. As students read, they ideally will add to their background knowledge so that they can better address what they were wondering. If students have a better understanding of illegal immigration, they will comprehend the anchor text, *Crossing the Wire*, more deeply. Giving students an opportunity to read a news article will also give me a chance to show them a reading strategy that will help them to be better readers of nonfiction.

Notice how each part of the workshop helps me

1. maximize time for students to do the work; and
2. assess, instruct, and differentiate for individual needs to ensure maximum learning for each student.

Day Two Workshop Focus: Questions Help Readers Build Background Knowledge and Sift and Sort Important Information in Nonfiction

When students enter the room, learning targets and assessments are written on the whiteboard:

Learning Targets	Assessments
I can select, read, and annotate a piece of nonfiction to build my background knowledge about a question I have.	annotated articles
I can record new background knowledge that I want to share with others.	response journals

7:20–7:35 Opening Structure

I welcome students and ask them to get out their novels and response logs. I remind them to read the learning targets written on the left side of the whiteboard.

On the other side of the whiteboard, I have written three provocative questions selected from students' work in the previous class. I make sure to credit the reader who asked the engaging question by writing his or her name at the end. I ask the class to read the questions and pick one they want to respond to. Students who don't find any of the questions interesting are instructed to write a question of their own and respond to it.

On the board:

- Why do people try to smuggle other people across the border? (Aaron)
- Why is being an illegal immigrant a crime? (Ricardo)
- Why are people here so against immigrants crossing the border? (Kaitlin)

  Option: If none of these questions appeal to you, write a question you care about and share your current thinking about it.

While students work on their responses, I take attendance and quickly check in with the students I conferred with during the previous class (see Figure 4.3). I touch base with Perla first. She finished the anchor text, *Crossing the Wire*, ahead of others in the class. During the previous class I invited her to choose a text from an immigration text set that I put together. (For each unit of study, I collect different titles and text structures on the topic. Text sets include picture books, novels, poetry anthologies, news clippings, nonfiction texts, letters, graphics, maps, political cartoons—anything that might increase students' background knowledge on the topic.) While students are responding to the questions on the board, I check in with Perla to see if the book she chose during the previous class is a good fit. She says she thinks it will be okay, but I can tell she is not thrilled with her selection. She has read only the first couple of pages, so I ask her to stick with the book for another ten pages and record any questions she has on sticky notes. I tell her I will try to help her answer those questions, but that if she is still struggling with the book after the additional ten pages, I'll help her make another choice. Perla smiles and says, "Okay."

I head to the front of the room to see how Isra's reading is going. She tells me she's been reading at night and got to page 50. "So far," she says, "I like the book." To check her comprehension, I ask her to tell me what she remembers reading. I can tell from what she says that she is understanding the basic plot of the story. This quick check tells me she can continue to read during the work time on her own.

At this point, I look around the room and see that almost everyone has written a response to one of the questions on the board. I ask a few students to share their responses. When they are finished, I move on to the mini-lesson. Today's opening went a little longer than usual. Instead of lasting ten minutes, it went about fifteen.

7:35–7:50 Mini-Lesson

When readers have a question about a topic in a novel they are reading, they can use nonfiction to build background knowledge and possibly answer their question. I begin the mini-lesson by sharing a question that I have about illegal immigration: "I am wondering what happens to students who are born in the United States to parents who are here illegally." A few students look at each other, but no one says a word. I continue, "Reading nonfiction can sometimes build my background knowledge so I can find answers to my questions. In order to find an article that will address my question, I have to look at the title and subheadings of each one to see which article will help me build my background knowledge in this area."

I show students the five articles I pulled from the Internet the previous day. (See Figure 4.7 to see the total collection of articles used in the immigration study.) I read the title of each article and ask the kids to help me decide, based on the title, which one might provide me with information about my question. We settle on one article, and I pass out a copy to everyone. I put my copy on the document camera so students can see how I read and annotate as I go. Before I start, I write my question about children born to undocumented immigrants at the top of the article. I do this to show students that my purpose for reading this particular article is to build background knowledge around this question. "Ideally," I say, "I will get my question answered. If I don't, I hope I'll learn something new that will make me smarter about illegal immigration."

Next, I model by reading aloud a small chunk of text. I stop and make a connection to a school in El Paso where I've done staff development work. Next, I jot a few notes about my thinking in the margins. I continue down the first column of the article, repeating this cycle of reading a section out loud, then thinking aloud, and finally, jotting down a few annotations.

After about four minutes of modeling what I want students to do on their own, I release the class to choose an article for themselves that they think will address a question they have. Students head to the table at the front of the room where the articles are arranged. Based on the individual questions they have, they read the title of each article and select one they think will build their background knowledge, so they can answer the question they are curious about. Once students have selected their text, they head back to their seats and begin reading and annotating.

7:50–8:00 Work Time

As the students get to work, I scan the classroom to see if everyone has an article. Next, I head over to Marcus to see if his glasses have been repaired (see Figure 4.3). I know that without them, he struggles to read for extended periods of time. Today, he has brought in the broken frames to show me why he hasn't been wearing them. The good news is that the frames aren't broken. They only need a screw. The bad news is that he can't find the lens. Marcus asks me to hold what is left of his glasses at school while he promises to look for the missing lens. It is imperative that he get his glasses back. In the meantime, I send him to the main office to see if someone can enlarge his copy of the article on the copy machine. Bigger print will make it easier for him to read for longer periods of time.

As Marcus leaves for the main office, I notice that Carlos appears to be daydreaming. I approach his desk. I kneel down and ask him how things are going. "Fine," he says.

"What is your article about?" I ask.

"Immigrants who came to the U.S. who invented cool stuff and now they are millionaires."

"Interesting," I say. "Is it helping you answer your question?"

"What question?"

"The question you have about illegal immigration."

"I don't have a question about illegal immigration."

I stand up from Carlos's desk and look around. I notice that no one in the area has a question written at the top of his or her paper. Obviously, my mini-lesson wasn't clear enough. Students didn't understand how important it is to have a question in mind when it comes to research and building background knowledge. It's no wonder they aren't digging into the reading. Many don't have a clear question, which means they don't have a way to sift and sort information.

8:00–8:03 Time for a Catch

In an attempt to efficiently remedy the situation, I decide to interrupt the work time by "catching" the class so that I can reteach this part of the mini-lesson. This catch is unplanned but very necessary. "Okay, guys, time out. I need to see how many of you have a question written at the top of your article. Raise your hand if you do." About four kids raise their hand. "Areonna, what is your question?" I ask.

"I want to know why it takes so long to get a visa."

"Great question. Adrianna, what is your question?"

"I want to know why Americans don't want Mexicans to come to the U.S."

"Terrific. Rodrigo, what are you wondering?"

"I want to know what drug smuggling has to do with illegal immigrants."

"Great questions, you guys." I point out to the class that their questions help them not only select an article but also determine what is important in the article. I instruct students who don't have a question at the top to write one down.

8:03–8:30 Work Time Resumes

Most of the kids get back to work, but I notice that a few of them are complaining. They are whining that they don't know what to ask. I decide to call a small group together to help them with this part of the lesson. These few students are stuck, and it is my job to help them get unstuck so they can get back to working on their own. "Anyone who doesn't have a question, meet me at the table in the front." Five kids get up and head to the table, bringing their articles. I release the rest of the class to resume working and head over to meet the kids who don't have a question.

8:03–8:15 Small Group

I gather the students around me and give each of them a sticky note. I explain that their goal is to walk away with at least one question they are wondering about when it comes to illegal immigration. I invite anyone from the group to share something they are thinking, and no one responds. So I start modeling. "Here's what I wonder," I begin. "How come illegal immigration is such a problem? Why don't we have the same problem with people emigrating from Canada? How come so many people from south of the U.S. border want to come to America? What is happening in Mexico and Central America to cause so many people to leave?"

Prompted by my models, Natalie asks, "I want to know why we can't let people stay here once they make it across the border."

"Great question, Natalie—write that down. Also take a look at the title and headings of the articles on the table and see if there is one that you think will give you some background knowledge on that question."

Labon then says, "I want to know more about the drugs and the people they call mules."

Figure 4.8

Conferring Notes

9/30

Invitational mini-lesson about coming up with a question to drive purpose for
reading nonfiction text. Modeled asking questions I care about to help choose a
text and give me a way to sift and sort important information.

   Next class, remember to check in with Natalie, Labon, Omar, James, Vanessa.

I hand him an article and say, "Here—this article might give you some
information about that topic. What about you, Omar? What are you
wondering?"

"How do kids who were born here but whose parents aren't legal get to
go to college?"

"Hmm . . . I don't know. I don't have an article about that topic specifically. Get on the computer in the corner and start researching. Try putting
in the search words *illegal immigrant* and *college* and see what you get. I'll
be over in a minute to see what you find."

James and Vanessa, the other two kids who didn't have a question, have
gone back to their seats. I wander over to them and see that they have
chosen an article. This time, though, they each have a question written at
the top. James wants to know why illegal immigration is such a big deal.
Vanessa wants to know more about the way people "cross." Everyone
appears to be on track. I have a bit of time left to check in with a few more
students. I peer over their shoulders to see how their thinking is going,
and then I write down a reminder of this small-group instruction in my
conferring notebook (see Figure 4.8).

At 8:30 I look at the clock and notice that if I don't wrap up the work
time, students won't have an opportunity to talk about what they have
read. Because it is early in the year, I must also make time to review how to
get into groups and how to discuss.

8:30–8:35 Planned Catch

I want students to get into groups of three or four. It doesn't matter if
people are all reading different articles. The purpose of the discussion is to
share background knowledge that they learned about immigration with
others in their group. The idea is that by sharing what they have read, they

Figure 4.9

Discussion Anchor Chart

Ways to discuss

- Take turns sharing.
- Ground your group members in the article by sharing a line from the text that struck you.
- Share your thinking by reading what you annotated in the margins.
- Before letting the next person share, give your group members an opportunity to respond to your comments.
- Group members might agree or disagree with you.
- They might ask a question or piggyback on something you said.
- When you have talked and your group has responded, ask, "Who wants to go next?"

---

will all get smarter. I instruct them to move their desks so they are facing each other. I also remind them to bring their annotated articles to the group. I can't assume that kids know what to do in a discussion group. I need to review norms quickly so they can begin discussing and debriefing what they read and learned. I draw their attention to an anchor chart we generated the week before and point out the different ways they might share their thinking. (See Figure 4.9.)

When readers and writers talk about their work, it helps them to understand it more deeply. I want the discussion groups to be productive; therefore, I need to plan on teaching them how to do it well. Most of the time I let students choose their own groups. I think it's an important skill to develop. Sometimes I have to intervene when a group isn't on task, but I have no problem moving people into different groups when this happens. It is also important to talk to people who aren't in one's "clique," so every third or fourth time we form discussion groups, I have kids count off so they have an opportunity to hear new thinking from people they don't typically talk to.

8:35–8:47 Debriefing: Small-Group Discussion

As students discuss, I move around the room with my group observation form and clipboard, capturing what students are saying. I record student quotes in the middle column of the sheet so I can share important thinking with the whole group. This gives me a chance to review content and shows students that their thinking matters. As I walk through the room, I hear Carlos say, "I have questions about this thing called NAFTA. What is it?"

Cindy jumps in with, "It's a treaty and was supposed to make things better for people in Mexico. I know it hasn't helped my family who lives there. My uncle lost his job because of it."

"How can a farmer lose his job?" asks Carlos. "I don't get the part about Mexican farmers being put out of jobs. Can't they just farm for their families?"

"No," says Javier. "Farming is expensive. You can't just farm and not get money. You need to get something for your crops or you go out of business."

As kids talk, I scribble as fast as I can. I try to capture their questions about NAFTA and their thinking about farming so that I can share it with the rest of the class. Getting them information on this topic will help them to better understand another reason why so many people from Mexico are trying to cross the border.

I head to the other side of the room. Ricardo has read about drug trafficking. He shares a couple of lines from his article and then tells the group his thinking about those lines. The group listens. He finishes, and no one says a word. They all stare at Ricardo, and I can tell he feels uncomfortable. It is clear that the kids in this group haven't had many opportunities to discuss their reading. I wait thirty excruciating seconds (while kids squirm in their seats) before modeling a response. "So, Ricardo," I say, "what struck you about what you just read?"

Ricardo starts to explain. "People who come here to make a better life are not bad people. It is the illegal immigrants who willingly smuggle drugs into the U.S. who are criminals. Those people should be deported," he says.

The rest of the group agrees, and then Natalie jumps in and says, "Yeah, but what about Victor and Rico in the book? They were forced to smuggle drugs. Should people like that also be deported?"

"No," says Kaitlin. "The people who just want to work to create a better life for their families should get to stay." With that, the group starts talking about the unfairness. I scribble a few notes before sharing with the whole class the group observation form. (See Figure 4.10.)

8:47–8:50 Whole-Group Debriefing— Sharing What I Saw and Heard

When kids debrief in groups, I try to save the last several minutes of class to share the group observation form. This formative assessment helps me

Figure 4.10 Group Observation Form

+	Quotes	−
■ Most students hold their thinking on their articles by annotating snippets of thought.		
■ Carlos asks a question.	"What is this thing called NAFTA?"	
■ Cindy responds to Carlos by giving him some information.	"It's a treaty and was supposed to make things better for people in Mexico."	
■ Rodrigo grounds his group by reading a part from the article.		
■ Labon keeps his group going by inviting someone else to share.	"Who would like to share next?"	
■ Vanessa accepts the invitation and shares what she says is her best piece of thinking.	"I never realized how big of an issue illegal immigration is."	Several people jump in and start talking all at once. Brainstorm ideas so that everyone's voice can be heard.
■ Ricardo shares a statistic from his article and then asks a question.	"Thirty percent of deportations have to do with crimes. Does that mean that only criminals are getting deported?"	No one responded to Ricardo. Show kids how to piggyback on someone's comment.

capture what I see and hear during the discussion time. In the left-hand (plus) column, I list what I see students doing well as readers, writers, and discussion participants. I point out that almost everyone in the class had annotations on their articles. "The thinking that you hold in the margins is a smart way to remember what was going through your mind as you read," I tell the class. I highlight Carlos's question about NAFTA and say, "Will Hobbs, author of *Crossing the Wire*, says this treaty has really increased the number of people who have illegally immigrated to the United States." I make a note to find something simple and succinct about NAFTA that I can share with the students. I point out how Cindy "piggy-backed" on Carlos's question by telling him what she knew about NAFTA. The middle column of the group observation form gives me a place to capture smart comments made by students and important pieces of content that have bubbled up as a result of their discussions.

Comments written in the right-hand (minus) column are areas that we need to work on the next time we get into discussion groups. I share that Ricardo's group left him hanging, and that we need to get better at "piggy-backing" on each other's comments.

Today, I don't get to record individual notes in my conferring notebook, but the small-group instruction that I was able to do was a fair trade for my time. If students understand that questions can propel them to read and research, my job will be easier all year long. Before stopping the group discussions for the whole-group debriefing, I quickly jot down in my notebook who joined the small group. I record a few notes about the modeling I did and a short note to remind myself whom to check in with during the next class period.

When the bell rings, I already have a pretty good idea of where I'll go next. I learn from the debriefing and discussion that students need more information on NAFTA. I learn from the small-group instruction that some students are still struggling to ask questions that they are truly curious about. I will read students' annotations tonight and learn more about the way they are holding their thinking in the margins. I will be able to see who needs more support when it comes to asking questions, choosing an article, reading the text, marking thinking, and discussing what they read. I am amazed by how much data I collect when I let kids do the work.

Plan for the Work Students Will Do

Over the course of writing this book, I was curious to know firsthand if the link I was making between the classroom and the athletic field was as strong as I thought. One afternoon, I asked a varsity basketball coach if he spent a lot of time planning his practices. He looked at me and said sarcastically, "I only plan when I don't want chaos."

No one wants to deal with chaos, especially in a classroom, but we know when we don't plan the right way, chaos ensues. The workshop model gives teachers a way to organize instruction and assessment so that students are the ones doing the work.

I learned from the conversations I had with coaches that the good ones don't talk during the whole practice time. If they did, their teams would never get better. Instead, successful coaches let the kids practice, and while kids are practicing, they assess and differentiate for players' needs. Sometimes they correct errors and bad habits. Other times they challenge players with more complex drills and plays. Coaches know that sometimes they have to reteach what they have modeled. They also know that they can use the athletes who have mastered the moves as exemplars for other players. As teams build more stamina and endurance and as they gain strength and skills, coaches introduce more and more sophisticated moves. They aren't afraid to go back and practice fundamentals, and they know they must regularly make time to reflect on what went well and what still needs to be practiced.

Planning and assessing with the workshop model in mind forces me to plan for student engagement. It ensures that I teach to my belief that whoever is doing the reading, writing, and talking is doing the learning. Most teachers I know can't work any harder than they already are. To make a dent in all they are asked to do, they have to work smarter, not harder. Harry Wong, former science teacher and now educational consultant, is quoted as saying, "School should not be a place where young people go to watch old people work." Sometimes, while seeing students exit at the end of an exhausting day, I am reminded of this quote. Watching them bound out the door, full of vim and vigor, chatting with friends and excited to get to the "good part" of their day, a tinge of martyrdom peppers my attitude. I think to myself, *Man, I wish I had energy like that.* When I hear myself saying this, I know it is time to regroup.

Instead of feeling sorry for myself, I head back to my room to rethink how I can make better use of my instructional time. I reflect on a few questions, asking myself, Who did the work today—my students or I? How well did I plan using the workshop model? Did my instruction lack planning so students' disengagement forced me to take over to restore order? Did I lecture the whole period, or did students get a chance to work?

Shifting the mind-set from planning what I'm going to do every minute of every class to what my students are going to be doing has dramatically increased student engagement. When I share class time with students, it is gratifying to know that even though they might not look tired when they leave, we have all put in a hard day of work.

What Works

Assessment Point: Effective assessors know that the purpose of assessment is to see if the instruction is working and students are learning. The workshop model makes it possible for teachers to plan for assessment. They know if they don't have a way to assess daily, students won't get the real-time feedback they need to improve.

Assessment Point: Effective assessors know it is important for students to have time to reflect on their learning every day. Reflections serve as another piece of evidence that helps teachers plan the following day's lesson. The debriefing is a great time to collect formative data. It doesn't have to be fancy. A sticky note with a student question on it can inform instruction just as much if not more than a common assessment. Effective assessors are always asking themselves, How will students show me their thinking so I can better plan for their needs tomorrow?

"Are You Up for a Challenge?"

1. Take advantage of all the different opportunities you have to assess and give feedback during workshop. Don't use work time to sit at your desk grading papers or checking e-mail. Use it to confer with your students and figure out where you need to go tomorrow. Notice patterns of confusion and understanding. Celebrate the successes and make note of the confusion so you can address it immediately or in the next day's mini-lesson. In your head, start planning tomorrow's mini-lesson. Do kids need a new skill, strategy, or process to work more independently? During the debriefing, let kids articulate what they think they have learned. Assess what they say and write it down so you will be smarter tomorrow about meeting their needs. Think of every minute of the workshop as an opportunity to assess and give feedback.

2. Make sure you don't skimp on time to debrief. This crucial component of the workshop model provides an opportunity for students to reflect on their learning. Regular opportunities to debrief not only hold students accountable for the way they use their work time, but also give teachers a second chance to assess what students need next. Allowing students to collect their thoughts at the end of the period and share new learning makes others in the class smarter. The debriefing also gives the teacher insight into students' patterns of understanding

and confusion. Consciously plan how students will synthesize and share their learning at the end of the period. Decide how you will bring the class back together to share. Will you debrief as a whole group, in small groups, or in pairs? Or will students reflect by themselves and share their learning through writing? You are the boss, so you decide.

CHAPTER 5

Annotations: A Trustworthy Source of Data

The conversation voice is like having a little man inside your head that narrates your thinking. I can manipulate this little man by having him ask questions about the text or have him chunk the reading and paraphrase ideas. Sometimes this little man decides to take a "walk" and he starts to think about something else other than the text. When this happens, I have to stop reading and send out a search party to get him back on track.

—*Rob, twelfth grade*

Quick and Informative

Often at the end of an in-service day, teachers are asked to complete an evaluation commenting on the presenter's effectiveness and their learning for the day. When I present, there is at least one teacher who has heard me before who is surprised by the fact that I don't have a whole new spiel. Just last month I received the following comment: "Thank you for the workshop. I have seen Cris before, and I am struck that she doesn't have lots of new activities or worksheets. It seems that she has a few core ideas that evolve over time." The teacher who wrote this comment hit the nail on the head. I don't have lots of new activities, and I prefer to call the ones that I do have anything but worksheets. The tools I share are ones that I use with students on a regular basis because they are manageable and guide my instruction. They also provide a convenient way for me to give students specific, descriptive feedback about their performance. I wrote extensively about the tools I use most often in my first two books, *I Read It, but I Don't Get It* (2000) and *Do I Really Have to Teach Reading?* (2004): inner-voice sheets, double-entry diaries, group observation forms, comprehension constructors, and reading response logs.

When deciding which formative assessment tool to use, I consider several questions:

- Can all learners use this tool to show thinking?
- Will this tool immediately inform my instruction and provide a way to give real-time feedback to students?
- Will patterns of understanding or confusion emerge as a result of using this tool?
- Is this tool convenient to design, use, and administer?

Giving a class of twenty-five to thirty students three or four questions to answer after reading a short piece of text is quick and easy to grade. Unfortunately, if there is only one right answer to the questions asked, student responses won't give me a lot of information about what they need to become better readers, writers, and thinkers. When students answer questions with one right answer, I don't get enough information about their comprehension to move them forward.

The most important assessment tool I use is also the simplest: I give students a piece of text and a compelling reason to read it, and ask them to annotate. Annotating a short article takes only about twelve minutes, but that twelve minutes of student work time tells me a lot about my students as learners. Let's take a look at an example of how annotations help assess students as readers.

What Does Kiana Know? What Does She Need?

From Kiana's annotations (Figure 5.1), I can tell a lot about the way she reads. Kiana has clearly read the article, but she is somewhat confused about what it says. I can tell she has miscued a part in the second section. She has read the line, "I think she'll sit down in prison and learn how to become a better criminal," but apparently is confused.

Kiana

Defiant teenager gets jail time in vehicular homicide

By Monte Whaley
Denver Post Staff Writer

Fort Collins — A 16-year-old girl got her wish Tuesday and was sentenced to adult prison for crashing her car into a duplex and killing a Loveland woman while fleeing police.

Stephanie Huff of Eaton will spend six years in a state prison after she failed to take part in any program in the state's Youth Offender System.

Huff was sentenced in April to the prison program for juveniles as part of a plea bargain reached with prosecutors for her part in the death of 28-year-old Shawna Rush. But Huff quickly made it clear to officials in the youth program that she wanted no part of what they had to offer, said Larimer County District Judge Daniel Kaup.

She wanted instead to go to prison. "Well, you get your wish," Kaup said.

Stephanie Huff, 16, killed a woman while fleeing police.

"To me, she doesn't even look like she wants to change," said Roy Rush, Shawna Rush's father. "I think she'll just sit right down in prison and learn to be a better criminal."

Huff said nothing at her sentencing. Public defender Stephen Sneider objected to the terms of the sentence, saying it violated an earlier agreement that would have netted Huff shorter prison time.

But Kaup said the sentencing matched what both sides in the cased agreed to after Huff pleaded guilty to car theft and vehicular eluding causing death.

Loveland police found Huff and a 14-year-old girl sleeping inside a stolen pickup in front of a private residence on Nov. 3.

After running a check and finding that Huff and the other girl were runaways, the officer returned to the pickup and told Huff that he'd have to take them into custody.

Huff sped off and crashed into a nearby duplex, killing Rush, who was inside.

Two days later, Huff stole a community corrections van that was transporting her and two other juveniles.

Huff also faces five years' probation after serving her prison sentence.

"This court has given her a chance, but she didn't give Shawna a chance," said Rush's sister, Nikki Basart.

[Handwritten annotations:]
what an idiot she wanted to go there... Why would she go there better yet. Why would she run away from the police.

- shes learning to be a better criminal?

-so she got in the car accident with a 14 yr old... What happened to the 14 yr old? -runaways...geez these girls are stupid -stole a community corrections van? shes dangerous...thats good shes in jail. I don't want her on the road...ever!

Figure 5.1
Kiana's
Annotations

Kiana has written at the bottom of this section, "She's learning how to be a better criminal?" The question mark leads me to believe that she is wondering why any adult would want a juvenile to learn how to be a better criminal. My guess is that she read the line, and as her eyes moved down the page, she continued thinking about her confusion. This happens a lot—to all readers, not just those who struggle. One minute they comprehend, and BOOM, the next minute something confusing has entered their brain and their thinking is pulled away from the words on the page. As their eyes continue down the text, their mind is still trying to figure out the part that was confusing.

I read Kiana's comments in the last column. I can tell she is confused, but based on what she wrote I don't think she knows she is confused. She has misread a few details, and because of this, she paraphrases what happened incorrectly. She adds a little editorial comment and is finished with the reading.

Kiana doesn't like to go back and reread when she gets confused. She gives herself one chance to get it and then moves on. As I think about how to help her, I try to prioritize what she needs *most*, right now.

For starters, I will praise her for recognizing her confusion in the second column. Next, I show her how to go back and reread the middle section with a specific purpose in mind. I will suggest a purpose and model that maybe she should go back and see if she can get an answer to her question about the adult wanting a kid "to sit down in prison and learn how to be a better criminal."

I will let Kiana know that she can reread with a different purpose, add more thinking under her original words, and then turn what she has back in for more points. Practice and do-overs will make Kiana a pro when it comes to interacting with and annotating text. This back-and-forth process is important: it helps me not only assess what Kiana needs, but name a strategy that I want to see her continue to use. Praising her for recognizing, admitting, and repairing her confusion encourages her to engage in this behavior again.

For me the hardest part of assessing comprehension is knowing how and what students think and need. Teachers can't see or hear what learners are doing in their heads the way they can see and hear athletes and musicians "perform." To differentiate instruction and move students to the next level of proficiency, I must give them ways to demonstrate understanding so that I can quickly assess where to go next. For years, I've asked students to annotate or hold their thinking in the margins of text or on sticky notes. This type of formative assessment immediately informs my instruction so I can help each student read better tomorrow than they did today.

Coding, Marking, or Annotating: What's the Difference?

Writing short margin notes to remember thoughts as one reads is nothing new. Over the past twenty years, I've referred to this technique in different ways: coding the text, marking thinking, and finally, annotating. As my thinking grew, I recognized that this strategy not only helps readers remember what they have read, but also serves as a powerful assessment tool to help teachers see what students think.

Thanks to Harvard University, I have settled on calling this formative assessment tool *annotation*. In a handout developed by Harvard's librarians, "Interrogating Texts: Six Reading Habits to Develop in Your First Year at Harvard," incoming freshmen are directed to "'Dialogue' with yourself, the author, and the issues and ideas at stake. From start to finish make your reading of any text thinking-intensive" (http://hcl.harvard.edu/research/guides/lamont_handouts/interrogatingtexts.html). The handout goes on to suggest several different ways to annotate the text. Simply put, annotating is a written record of how readers think *as* they read instead of *after* they read.

Annotated margins help the teacher see which students are reading, how they are thinking, who has an insight, who is struggling, and who needs immediate help. When I read what my students annotate, I can see entry points for instruction and immediately know how to give students feedback. At the beginning of the school year when I am working especially hard to learn who my students are as readers, writers, and thinkers, it is important that the feedback I give not shut down anyone's thinking. If I respond in a way that discourages thinking, students are less willing to take a risk. This can encourage them to cheat or fake their responses, which means I lose a valuable opportunity to assess their thinking. For this reason, I always try to find something that a student has done well that I can point out as my beginning platform for feedback. (In Chapter 6, I discuss more specifically how I give feedback.)

When readers annotate, they have a purpose for their reading. Therefore they are less likely to let their eyes move down the page while their mind wanders. This is important, because many learners tell me at the beginning of the year that when they don't choose or like the reading material, they have trouble remembering what they have read. When readers annotate, they can tell by their annotations if their mind is interacting with the text or has wandered onto another topic. The inability to annotate something related to the reading alerts learners that their minds have wandered, which gives them an opportunity to go back and reread before their thoughts stray too far from the text.

Annotating is a way for readers to hold their thinking in all subject areas and at all grade levels. Students can be taught to annotate at any age. The technique isn't dependent on a reader's ability to write well, either. Even first graders can annotate, using pictures or symbols that represent their questions or connections. Unlike tools that have only one right answer, such as a pop quiz or questions at the end of a chapter, annotating provides a way for readers to show their thinking even if they don't completely understand.

From annotations, teachers can see who is falling behind in their reading. They can also tell who hasn't read at all. "Faked" annotations are obvious, but even that gives the teacher insight into the learner. Cheating is also discouraged when students are asked to annotate, because there is more than one right answer. If two students have the exact same annotations, the teacher knows that one person thought and the other person copied.

The more ways students have to think about text, the more proficient at reading they will become. When students annotate, I can see who has the "conversation voice" turned on inside their head, actively engaging with the text. Unfortunately, unless shown by their teachers, many adolescent readers don't know how to have a conversation with a primary document, textbook, or Victorian-era novel. Students need to see different ways to annotate different text structures. When teachers take time to demonstrate how they annotate their discipline's text, they not only give readers the words they need to engage their thinking as they read, but also show students how to read strategically. When students know how to annotate, it gives their teachers a record of their thinking that informs the next day's instruction.

Getting Kids to Annotate: Where Do I Start?

Because student annotation is such an important part of my assessment practice, I start teaching kids how to do it during the first days of class. Initially I show them what it looks like to "talk back" to the text. When I model, I want to demonstrate for students different ways to interact and think when they read. When students begin annotating, they sometimes say, "I don't know what to write." Often, the first type of annotation I model is how to ask questions about the reading.

Asking questions to which I don't know the answers is a strategy that helps me interact with difficult text. When I annotate questions in the margins of my reading, I have a better chance of sticking with challenging reading material. Questions propel me to read on, and when I encounter difficulty, asking a question can help me isolate my confusion. When I model authentic questions that I have on the first read, I start to break students of the habit of thinking that it is the teacher's job to ask all the questions and the students' job to answer them. Figure 5.2 is an example of "model" annotations that I shared in a mini-lesson during the first weeks of school.

After I did a think-aloud with the first two columns of text, pausing to write my annotations along the way, I asked students to continue annotating the article. Figure 5.3 is the same article annotated by a student. Chris's annotations tell me that he knows how to ask questions to which he doesn't know the answer, that he feels empathy for the issue, and that he is trying to solve problems as he reads. I infer that Chris can read more challenging text than this, so I need to find out what he is curious about when it comes to the topic of immigration and steer him in that direction. I need to make sure he is continually challenged so he can continue to grow as a reader.

Generally I learn more from the questions students ask than from the answers they give. If I can get students to ask questions that they are truly

Figure 5.2
Model
Annotations

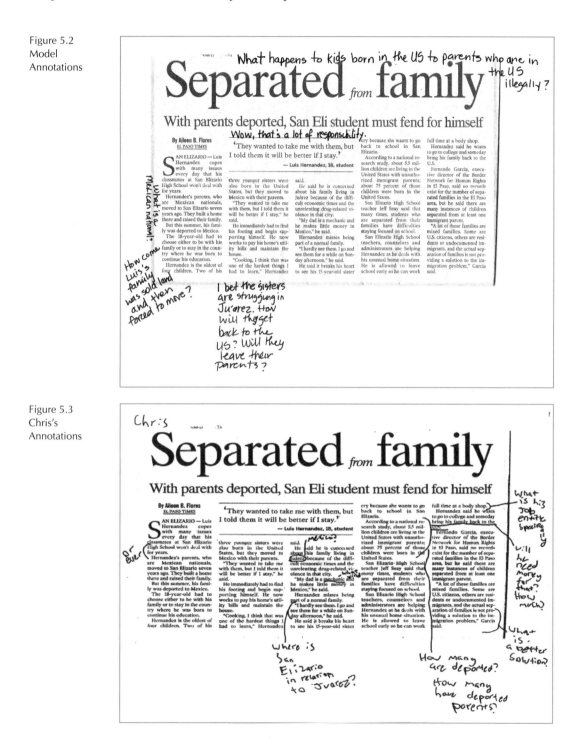

Figure 5.3
Chris's
Annotations

curious about, I not only see where their knowledge gaps are, but can also show them a way to stay engaged with difficult text. From the beginning, I want to crush the idea that there is only one way to have a conversation when reading.

At the beginning of the year, I struggle to get kids to ask questions they care about. In this era of standardized testing, many students have been conditioned to think that every question should have a neat answer. I want learners to recognize that there is ambiguity in the world, and I reassure them that the best questions don't always have answers—or certainly not the same answer. Sometimes by just nodding and saying, "Wow, that's an interesting question" or writing back to students, "You should share that question with your discussion group," I honor the ambiguity that big questions deserve. I want them to see that the only way to get over the "I don't know" hump is to ask a question.

Below is an anchor chart my students and I started to document how the strategy of asking questions helps readers engage with text (Figure 5.4).

Another way to make thinking visible is to use student annotations as models to help others see what I want. If I am trying to teach students how to ask better questions, I look for questions that students have left me from their work that day. I record several of them on chart paper or on a handout so I can share them during the opening structure of the next workshop. Often I do this when we are starting a new unit of study or a new novel. I want students to know that good readers often have lots of questions at the beginning of a book. Authors want readers to wonder and be curious so that they'll keep reading. Students sometimes get discouraged when they have a lot of questions and assume that the book is too hard for them. Often when self-doubt sets in, they immediately want to abandon the text. I can honor thinking and reassure them that their questions are important by highlighting what they have asked the following day. At the same time, I can use their questions as models for kids who aren't sure what I want them to do.

Figure 5.4

Anchor Chart: How Questions Help Readers

When readers ask questions, they . . .

- create a purpose for themselves to keep reading;
- have a way to sift and sort information;
- set themselves up to think inferentially;
- can isolate their confusion; and
- give themselves a way to "talk back" to the text so their minds don't wander.

Figure 5.5

What Are You Wondering?

(Class questions as of October 10—pp. 1–11)

- What is Hate Week? (Sam)
- What is INGSOC? (Grant)
- What do the Thought Police do? (Tory)
- What does love have to do with "law and order"? (Jean)
- If there are no laws, how does the government control people? (Jon, Justin)
- Did the government get rid of calendars, watches, and the way time is measured? (Sarah, Jasna)
- Why can't Party Members go into ordinary shops? (Ashley, Dominique)
- Why are people cheering for gruesome deaths? (Patrick, Steffi)
- Why are liquor and cigarettes named "victory gin and cigarettes"? (Nikki, Alex, Joey)
- What is a forced labor camp? (Kelly)
- Why would the Ministry of Love need barbed wire? (Jeff, China)
- Why did the telescreen in Winston's room move? (Sharlotta)
- Why is it bad to write in a journal? (Jennie)
- Is Winston a bad guy? (Elizabeth)
- Who is the brown-haired girl? (Rob)

Figure 5.5 is an example of an initial question anchor chart generated from students' questions after reading the first few pages of *1984*. I record these questions on an anchor chart so others in the class can see that they aren't the only ones wondering what is going on. Not every student has thinking represented on the chart, because some of them didn't ask any questions.

Whenever I create an anchor chart with students' thinking on it, I record the thinking and the name of the student responsible. For the students who don't share, I want to find out why. In the case of *1984*, some students reported later that they had thought that if they asked a question, they would have to answer it.

This anchor chart initially serves as a support for the kids who didn't ask any questions. It is also a way of holding students accountable. It says, "Questions matter and we need everyone's thinking in order to figure out what this book is about." I date and save this anchor chart. We return to the initial questions anchor chart after completing the novel, because it is gratifying to examine which questions got answered, which ones were important to the work, and which ones were irrelevant. Students have a tangible artifact that shows how they got smarter.

Annotating Stumbling Blocks

Sometimes when I suggest that student annotations can be used as a formative assessment tool, teachers have some concerns. Following are some of the comments I hear most often. I've included some suggestions on how I've addressed these issues.

"My students can't write in their books."

Students' annotations are typically done on articles or something that is copied. When it comes to schoolbooks, most of the time students can't write directly on the text. When I want them to annotate thinking on text that they can't write on directly, I give them sticky notes to use. Readers are instructed to place the sticky notes next to the section of text that caused their thinking. On the sticky notes, they record their questions, connections, paraphrases, new thinking, and opinions. When students place their sticky notes so that the edge is hanging over the side, they can return to their reading later to easily recall what was happening in their head as they read.

When students use sticky notes to show thinking, I need an easy way to assess what they are doing without taking the books out of their hands. Sifting and sorting tons of sticky notes is laborious and time consuming. So instead of lugging baskets of books home on the weekends and spending hours going through hundreds of sticky notes, I have started asking students to self-select the ones they want to share with me. I ask them to record the page numbers on the sticky notes they select and then neatly arrange them all on a single sheet of notebook paper so they are easy for me to assess. Usually I ask for ten pieces of thinking, but teachers can decide on the number that works best for them. Sometimes the notes they share represent their best thinking. Other times, they represent their only recorded thinking. Either way, it culls out the less important sticky notes so that I can better manage how I assess and grade what they have done up to a certain point.

Once students have self-selected their sticky notes, I can quickly go through and assess comprehension, give feedback, or give points for their work. I can also use some sticky notes as models for the opening section of workshop during the next class.

Figures 5.6 and 5.7 are two examples of notebook pages filled with students' sticky notes. Both students are seniors who were reading Simon Wiesenthal's *The Sunflower*, a compelling and challenging read that gives students an opportunity to think about forgiveness and redemption.

Because this novel is so challenging to read, it gives me an opportunity to model thinking strategies that will help readers construct meaning. Students get lots of practice consciously applying thinking strategies as they work to repair confusion and make personal meaning from the text. This anchor text gives them valuable practice with learning how to stick with difficult reads that they will encounter the following year and beyond.

Figure 5.6 shows Matt's annotations as he read *The Sunflower*. Matt is a struggling reader who has experienced a great deal of hardship in his life. He isn't the best student when it comes to study habits, but he has regular attendance and works hard in class. *The Sunflower* is difficult for him to read, but because of his annotations I can tell where he is struggling. Interestingly, his personal connections help him understand the theme of "man's inhumanity to man" as exemplified in this work of Judaica. Even though he doesn't get every plot point, he seems to understand the big ideas around forgiveness and redemption. Matt is not grade driven. He just wants to pass the class so he can graduate. For him to do this, he needs to ask questions and admit confusion when he is stuck. I can best serve him by showing him how to repair his confusion so he will be a better reader the next time he encounters difficulty.

Figure 5.7 shows Stephanie's annotations. She sports a 4.0 GPA and is highly proficient at playing the game of school. She is a lovely student and works hard to give any teacher just what he or she wants. She understands the plot and can retell what she has read on a literal level. However, because she is so grade driven, she is hesitant to infer or to risk constructing personal meaning. Stephanie sticks with safe responses and does what she can to mask her confusion.

When I look at the thinking that Matt and Stephanie have chosen to turn in for points and feedback, I notice a difference in how the two respond. I am struck by Matt's ability to relate to Simon's story. He seems to understand the conflict the protagonist feels when asked to grant forgiveness to the Nazi officer on behalf of all the murdered Jews the officer confesses to have killed.

Stephanie, on the other hand, has a lot more thinking recorded than Matt does. She has three pages filled with large sticky notes, whereas Matt has only one page of small ones. Yet, nothing that Stephanie has written is new thinking for her. Her sticky notes are repetitive. She asks one question that she later answers for her group with a definite "No, God never takes time off." I get the sense that she is trying to please me and write something that I want to read. My goal for Stephanie before the semester ends is to help her be more of a selfish reader. Instead of reading for other people or the "one right answer," Stephanie needs to construct personal meaning.

Figure 5.6
Matt's
Annotations

Matt

| is there something that cannot be forgiven? | What's the deal with the sunflower | Don't they feel betrayed by God? pg. 8 |

| is he questioning's God's Faith? p.g. 9 | are some Germans choosing Favorites? | The more they work the less there likely to die? |

| Doesn't that give them a trembling feeling a band playing when you know your going to die? | Why didn't he leave? when he heard all of this? | What's going to happen to him? is he going to get killed |

| What happened to the nazi soldier? p.12 | where there times when he Just wanted the nazi to die? | what's going through his mind while he's telling him these things? |

| Did he really want to stay and listen to him? | what does he mean by mysticism superstition in this situation | why didn't the nazi stand up for what he believed in? |

| | How cruel, why would they do such a thing | |

When I ask students to choose their annotations, it forces them to determine what is important. It gives them ownership of their thinking and allows them to decide what they want me to assess. By having them put the sticky notes on a piece of notebook paper, I can provide some feed-

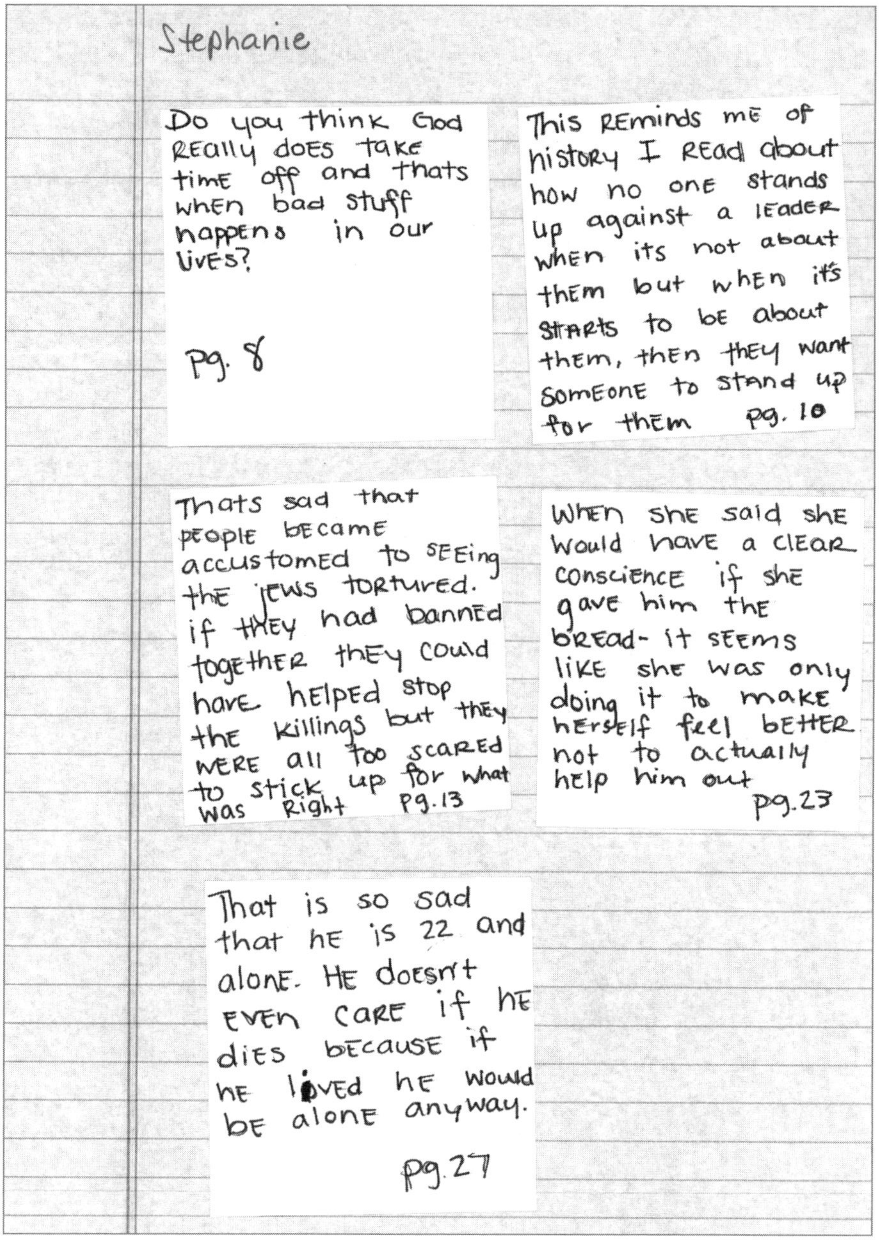

Figure 5.7
Stephanie's
Annotations

Stephanie

Do you think God REALLY does take time off and thats when bad stuff happens in our lives?

pg. 8

This REMINDS mE of history I REAd about how no one stands up against a lEadER when its not about thEm but whEn it's stRARts to bE about them, then they want somEonE to stand up for them   pg. 10

Thats sad that pEoplE bEcamE accustomEd to sEEing the jEws toRtuREd. if thEy had bannEd togethER thEy could have hElpEd stop the killings but thEy wERE all too scaREd to stick up for what was Right   pg. 13

WhEn shE said shE would have a clEaR conscience if she gave him the bREad- it sEEms likE she was only doing it to makE herself feEl bEttER not to actually help him out   pg.23

That is so sad that hE is 22 and alonE. HE doesn't EvEn caRE if hE dies bEcausE if he lovEd hE would bE alonE anyway.

pg. 27

back and also easily lift a note or two the next day and place it on the document camera to share models of thinking with the rest of the class. Sometimes the sticky notes that I share are examples of thinking that will help others understand the text more deeply. Other times, I share how a student uses strategic thinking to construct meaning or go beyond plot. I never share an annotation that would embarrass a student. When it comes to student work samples, I only share examples that highlight something positive.

Sticky notes make annotating *all* text possible. In addition, they offer flexibility when it comes time to give feedback.

"Some students won't annotate."

Most people don't wake up in the morning and hope that they'll be big failures all day long. One of my core teaching beliefs is that all students want to be successful and that students would be if they could be. When students don't annotate, it is often because they don't know what I want or what I mean. Some learners struggle because they are used to answering questions, not sharing their thinking. They have learned from years of experience that their job is to figure out what the teacher is thinking and regurgitate it. These kids don't know what I mean when I say, "You're the reader. Your thinking matters most."

When students refuse to annotate, I have two plans of attack. The first plan is to model more. Because the whole class doesn't need it, I usually do the modeling in a conference during work time. I kneel down beside the struggling annotator's desk and ask, "So, what are you thinking?" Sometimes students tell me what's happening in their heads as they read, and I quickly write down what they've said in the form of an annotation. Then I say, "Try a couple more and I'll be back in a few minutes to see what you have." This tiny bit of attention helps them dig in, because they know I'm coming back. The combination of attention and accountability is just enough to engage some readers.

Other times, kids who resist annotating tell me that they aren't thinking at all. When this happens, it's my cue to model what I want them to do. First, I read a short chunk of text out loud and then share what I'm thinking. Next, I jot my annotation on the text or sticky note so they can see that they don't have to write a lot. I repeat the process once or twice and then say, "Okay, now it's your turn. I will read a little bit aloud, and then you tell me what you're thinking." After students share what they think, I act as their secretary, recording their words in the margins. Usually after a couple of tries, they are ready to try it on their own.

During the debriefing, I make sure to touch base with the students who were struggling to see if I can give them some useful feedback. Often the feedback comes in the form of specific praise. For example, I might say, "David, you asked a question that didn't have an easy answer. Will you please share it with the class so they can think about it as well?"

Praising how David annotated and then using him as a model for the rest of the class goes a long way when it comes to giving reticent annotators confidence.

Another plan for encouraging resistant annotators is to point out its practicality. I explain that annotating is an easy way for them to show me where they are stuck and what they understand. This helps me be more effective when it comes to meeting their needs. "My job," I tell them, "is to help you be a better reader, writer, and thinker. Your job is to show me that you're thinking so I know what you need." I point out that I can give them quizzes or assign questions for them to answer at the end of chapters. However, both ways are sometimes unfair, because sometimes students do the work or complete the reading and still fail the quiz or assignment. Quizzes and end-of-chapter questions invite cheating because they don't allow for divergent thinking. Students can copy the answers, and then teachers don't know what they need until it is too late.

Readers who do read but don't fully comprehend usually struggle when it comes time to take a quiz. When they do poorly, the teacher has no way of knowing why. The incorrect answers on the quiz don't give the teacher any information about how to help the learner. Students who do comprehend but read for a purpose different from that of the teacher aren't able to have their thinking honored either, because they are asked to share it in only one way. Annotations are a way for students and teachers to work together. Students can be honest about their thinking so that teachers have a better chance of differentiating their instruction.

Sometimes some learners just need a little more convincing than others that annotating is useful. Last spring, a group of students were really fighting me when it came to annotating text. No matter what I said, I couldn't convince them that recording their thinking in the margins would help them construct meaning. I was starting to doubt the power of annotating, when in fact, I hadn't been explicit enough about its benefits. I went home that evening and jotted down how annotations had helped me as a reader and as a teacher. During the next class, I shared what I had written and was amazed at how my honest reflection persuaded them to buy into the process. (See Figure 5.8.)

Some students don't recognize a need to annotate until they see how it benefits not only the teacher but themselves as well. When students understand that I don't have to give as many quizzes or assign sets of comprehension questions when they annotate, they are much more likely to engage. I also find that when struggling readers learn that I'm not looking for one way to think about the reading, they are more likely to share their thinking in annotations. Before too long, most students find this tool so helpful that they use it without even being asked.

Figure 5.8 Why Bother to Annotate?

It helps readers . . .	It helps the teacher . . .
■ engage with the text when their minds are tempted to wander.	■ distinguish who is actually reading and who is "fake" reading.
■ hold thinking so it can be referred to later.	■ "see" what strategies readers are using to access meaning.
■ recall thinking so they can share with an expert what they need.	■ diagnose what learners need in order to better comprehend the text.
■ remember what they thought was important at the time of the reading.	■ assess what learners understand about the content and how they determinine what is important.
■ notice patterns, synthesize new thinking, and ask questions to build more background knowledge.	■ notice how the reader is using strategies to construct personal meaning.

Other Annotation Applications

Annotating as a viable assessment opportunity is easy to dismiss because it is so simple to use. Yet I continue to use this instructional strategy as my number-one source of trustworthy data, mainly because it puts learners in the driver's seat when it comes to showing me what they understand. Below are three more ways to use annotating as an assessment:

1. Annotations as a Pretest

Asking students to annotate thinking at the beginning of a unit is an efficient way to assess what they know and what skills and information they need. Sometimes when working with math and science teachers, I ask learners to annotate the chapter test the day we *start* the unit. Students are instructed to do their best. This means that they should solve the problems or answer the questions they can. Questions or problems they can't solve need to have an annotation next to them so that teachers can gain some insight into student needs. Typical annotations include connections to previous chapters or questions about big concepts. Sometimes students will partially work a problem or answer only a portion of a question because they get stuck. When they get to this juncture, they are instructed to isolate their confusion by asking a question. These annotations help the teacher figure out what is causing difficulty for the student so he or she can better target what the student needs.

Colleagues who try this quickly discover that there are some concepts and skills that the entire class needs. They also learn that some of the material can be skipped because everyone already knows it. The best part of using annotations as a pretest is that it helps teachers know where they need to differentiate their instruction. Analyzing what students know and don't know from the pretests will make it much easier for teachers to form small groups for enrichment or targeted intervention.

From the annotated pretests, teachers can also form small groups that will allow them to build skills and concepts that they know some students will need. Small-group work then takes place during the work time of workshop. While the rest of the class is working on its own, teachers can call up different groups of students based on specific needs.

Sometimes I call up a group of students who need more modeling. Other times I call a group together who just need a little more practice with me close by to coach. There are also instances when some students need intensive instruction to keep up with the rest of the class. Knowing what different groups of students need helps me use class time to differentiate instruction. When I don't have to waste time teaching skills that students already know, I can spend more time teaching them something new.

2. Annotations Lay the Groundwork for Real-Time Feedback.

Annotated thoughts in the margins of texts are gold mines of thinking. Teachers can see questions and connections that allow them to assess readers' levels of background knowledge and understanding. When misconceptions arise, teachers can quickly detect them and begin reteaching the concept. Reading and quickly responding to students' annotations is much more preferable to grading the same answer to the same question time and time again. I can actually say that I like grading student annotations. I'm sure that it has to do with the way they invite independent thought and divergent thinking.

I don't respond to every annotation, only the ones that provide an entry point for useful feedback. Typically I reply to only two to five annotations, depending on how long the assignment is. Sometimes the feedback is about improving the way a student uses a thinking strategy. Other times I add a bit of information that deepens the student's knowledge about the topic of study. Sometimes I ask a question to push deeper. On some occasions, I clarify or answer a question that a student has asked. I can also name or give specific praise about the way a student has demonstrated thinking in hopes that he or she will do it again.

Timely feedback not only increases students' knowledge about the topic, it also improves how metacognitively they read. When students are taught that their annotations need to connect to the text in some way, they can use what they write to monitor their comprehension. For example, an annotation that has nothing to do with the topic is often a signal to the reader that his mind has wandered or confusion has set in. Annotating serves as a check for the reader, but it also allows the teacher to see how to scaffold students' understanding. I reassure students that I rarely understand everything I read the first time around. Feedback often gives students another opportunity to revisit the text and grow their understanding.

When students know the goal isn't to answer questions but to increase comprehension, they are more apt to engage in the process of reading. By not looking for and rewarding one "right" answer, teachers can honor students' attempts to construct meaning. Providing quick feedback to students' annotations supports student thinking about the content. In a short time, this symbiotic relationship leads students and teachers to work together as co-constructors of meaning.

Changing how we ask students to show understanding, from answering questions to annotating text, emphasizes a more accurate view of how comprehension occurs. Responding to students' annotations emphasizes that comprehension is a process: meaning does not arrive; it has to be constructed.

3. Annotations and Targeted Mini-Lessons

Annotations are instrumental in helping teachers plan their mini-lessons for upcoming workshops. When I want to check comprehension quickly and figure out what kids need next to make sense of their reading, I copy a couple of pages out of a text that they have previously been assigned. I explain that I am doing a comprehension check and want to see what they understand and what is causing them confusion. Depending on the size of the text, I give them a specific number of annotations that I want them to shoot for. I explain that it is important for them to show me not only how they are thinking, but what they understand.

From their annotations, I can see different strategies that students use to construct meaning. I can also see where I need to shore up their thinking. Often these comprehension checks give me several different options for mini-lessons that I can choose to teach during the following class.

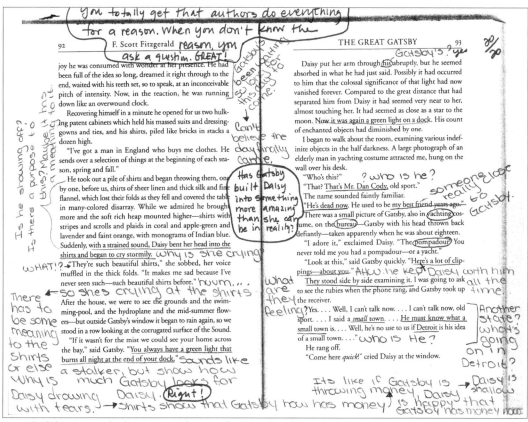

Figure 5.9
Sample Student
Annotations

In Figure 5.9, students are in the midst of reading *The Great Gatsby*. I want not only to help these juniors understand this challenging text better, but to help them improve their reading and writing skills. As I read what they have written, I look for patterns of confusion and places of understanding. I also try to respond to three or four of their annotations. Sometimes I answer a question they have asked. Other times I ask a question about something they have written. I explain unknown vocabulary words if I can, and sometimes I ask them to clarify what they mean. While I am giving feedback, I start a list, collecting possible mini-lessons that I can teach during the next class period.

Based on what I learned from their annotations, I design the following workshop components:

Opening: I want students to think about some of the dreams and goals they've had. Students will relate better to Gatsby's character if they can connect to a time in their life when they have dreamed of something for so long that

Aimee

20/20

F. Scott Fitzgerald   92

Gatsby is in awe
Cant believe he's finally with her again.

joy he was consumed with wonder at her presence. He had been full of the idea so long, dreamed it right through to the end, waited with his teeth set, so to speak, at an inconceivable pitch of intensity. Now, in the reaction, he was running down like an overwound clock.

Recovering himself in a minute he opened for us two hulking patent cabinets which held his massed suits and dressing-gowns and ties, and his shirts, piled like bricks in stacks a dozen high.

"I've got a man in England who buys me clothes. He sends over a selection of things at the beginning of each season, spring and fall."

that's a bit dramatic. I think Gatsby is trying to show off his wealth to Daisy.

He took out a pile of shirts and began throwing them, one by one, before us, shirts of sheer linen and thick silk and fine flannel, which lost their folds as they fell and covered the table in many-colored disarray. While we admired he brought more and the soft rich heap mounted higher—shirts with stripes and scrolls and plaids in coral and apple-green and lavender and faint orange, with monograms of Indian blue. Suddenly, with a strained sound, Daisy bent her head into the shirts and began to cry stormily.

Why did she react that way? She's weird.

"They're such beautiful shirts," she sobbed, her voice muffled in the thick folds. "It makes me sad because I've never seen such—such beautiful shirts before."

After the house, we were to see the grounds and the swimming-pool, and the hydroplane and the mid-summer flowers—but outside Gatsby's window it began to rain again, so we stood in a row looking at the corrugated surface of the Sound.

"If it wasn't for the mist we could see your home across the bay," said Gatsby. "You always have a green light that burns all night at the end of your dock."

Creepy much? a little
Sounds like a stalker yes—
How do people make decisions when they are obsessed with someone.

THE GREAT GATSBY   93

Admitted too much

Daisy put her arm through his abruptly, but he seemed absorbed in what he had just said. Possibly it had occurred to him that the colossal significance of that light had now vanished forever. Compared to the great distance that had separated him from Daisy it had seemed very near to her, almost touching her. It had seemed as close as a star to the moon. Now it was again a green light on a dock. His count of enchanted objects had diminished by one.

At first, the significance of the green just gave Gatsby hope that one day they would finally meet again. now that it happened he won't have to gaze at it the same way as hopeful.

I began to walk about the room, examining various indefinite objects in the half darkness. A large photograph of an elderly man in yachting costume attracted me, hung on the wall over his desk. *Could he have been in "business" with Gatsby? yes*

"Who's this?"
"That? That's Mr. Dan Cody, old sport." *Right!*
The name sounded faintly familiar.
"He's dead now. He used to be my best friend years ago."
There was a small picture of Gatsby, also in yachting costume, on the bureau—Gatsby with his head thrown back defiantly—taken apparently when he was about eighteen.

its becoming obvious that he's trying to hide things

"I adore it," exclaimed Daisy. "The pompadour! You never told me you had a pompadour—or a yacht."

"Look at this," said Gatsby quickly. "Here's a lot of clippings—about you."

They stood side by side examining it. I was going to ask to see the rubies when the phone rang, and Gatsby took up the receiver.

I think he plans to move.

"Yes. . . . Well, I can't talk now. . . . I can't talk now, old sport. . . . I said a *small* town. . . . He must know what a small town is. . . . Well, he's no use to us if Detroit is his idea of a small town. . . ."

He rang off.

"Come here *quick*!" cried Daisy at the window.

maybe too much gossip has been said about him and doesn't want to get caught?

Reprinted with the permission of Scribner, a Division of Simon & Schuster, Inc., from *The Great Gatsby* (Authorized Text) by F. Scott Fitzgerald. Copyright © 1925 by Charles Scribner's Sons. Copyright renewed © 1953 by Frances Scott Fitzgerald Lanahan. All rights reserved.

Figure 5.10
Aimee's
Annotations

the dream is better than reality could ever be. I direct their attention to page 95 and read aloud the excerpt below. While I take attendance, I ask students to reflect in their journals on the question, "What happens when dreams exceed reality?"

> *There must have been moments even that afternoon when Daisy tumbled short of his dreams—not through her own fault, but because of the colossal vitality of his illusion. It had gone beyond her, beyond everything.*

After students have had a chance to reflect, I share Aimee's annotations (Figure 5.10). I point out that she has asked questions about parts she doesn't understand. I also show how she has annotated her thinking throughout the passage. This takes about four minutes.

Mini-lesson: During the previous class, I noticed a pattern of confusion in the annotations students made when there was dialogue. Based on those, I decide to do a mini-lesson showing how authors use dialogue to reveal character traits. I'm hoping that pointing this out will clear up their confusion. In addition, knowing that authors use dialogue to tell readers who their characters are will help them be better readers not only of *The Great Gatsby* but of all novels. I highlight how F. Scott Fitzgerald uses what Gatsby and Daisy say to show readers what they care about and what is important to them. I model how I infer from their words and actions who they are as people. I do this several times, and then I ask them to find a place in the text where characters are talking.

David raises his hand and refers us to page 92, when Daisy is crying over Gatsby's European, handmade shirts. He reads the lines, "'They're such beautiful shirts,' she sobbed, her voice muffled in the thick folds."

David looks up from his book and says, "Wow, she is shallow. I think from these words that Daisy only cares about material things. I don't think she really loves Gatsby. I don't understand why she would cry about it, though."

"Hmm . . . That's an interesting question, David. What do you suppose Fitzgerald wants us to think about Daisy after we read that she is crying over Gatsby's handmade shirts?"

"I think she's an idiot. Does Fitzgerald want us to think she's an idiot?"

"Perhaps. As a reader you get to decide. What would you think of a girl who cried over your shirts?"

"I would think that all she cared about was the way I dressed."

"Great job, David." I turn to the rest of the class. "Did you notice how David took what Daisy said and how she acted to infer what she's like as a person?" At this point, I send students off to work on their own. While they are reading and annotating, I am conferring with and modeling for kids who need my help.

Work time: For the next forty minutes, students are instructed to read wherever they are in *The Great Gatsby*. They are to find five instances of dialogue and mark those places with a sticky note. On the sticky note, they are to jot down a few inferences about what the dialogue says about the characters as people.

Catch: When I find an excellent example from a student who has matched a piece of dialogue with a logical inference, I call the class together for a brief sharing. I do this to reinforce what was modeled in the mini-lesson.

Debriefing: During the debriefing, students form groups of four or five and share their sticky notes. Before students leave for the day, I send them back to their journals to record what they've learned from the dialogue about Gatsby and Daisy.

No Such Thing as the Perfect Mini

There is no such thing as a perfect mini-lesson. There are several needs that I could have addressed based on student annotations that day. I can't wait for a pacing guide to tell me what to teach. I have to base my instruction on students' immediate needs. Over time, I will address as many needs as possible, but each day I must prioritize what I think students need most. I also know that I have the work time each day to attend to individual needs through conferring.

Figure 5.11 is a chart of possible mini-lessons that I could have taught the following day. Obviously some are more important than others. Based on the annotations students left, these are the choices of mini-lessons I hope to deliver over time.

Annotations are data that give me a direction for my instruction. They are not a "final" demonstration of comprehension, but a jumping-off point. They help me have conversations with students about making meaning and growth over time.

Annotating in Different Disciplines

Earlier in the chapter, I mentioned the handout that Harvard University shares with its incoming freshmen. I share this handout with my students and point out the part that asks readers to "dialogue with the issues and ideas at stake." When readers know how to "talk back" to text, they take ownership of how they are thinking when they read. Talking back to text forces readers to interact with the words on the page and begin to construct meaning. Unfortunately many of my students don't know how to have a conversation with certain disciplinary texts, and therefore, their minds start to wander when they read the words. I recognize that I'm not an expert, either, when it comes to conversing with all specialized text. To help my students become better readers of text outside of my content area, I decide to interview colleagues in other disciplines and ask them how they interact with the texts they require their students to read.

I start off by selecting colleagues who teach the International Baccalaureate and Advanced Placement courses. My reasoning for interviewing these teachers is that their students are asked to read the most sophisticated texts in the building. If they can share strategies that will help their students become better readers, it stands to reason that students of less sophisticated text will also benefit. Once I have selected the teachers from specific disciplines, I instruct them to choose a challenging

Figure 5.11 Possible Mini-Lessons from One Day of Students' Annotations

Skills/Strategies	Vocabulary	Questions related to the novel	Information needed to be a better reader of literature
Quotation marks and paragraphing help the reader know who is talking.	■ love nest ■ billow ■ pompadour ■ boarder ■ scanty ■ colossal	What is the significance of the song on page 95? Do students understand that the words in italics are lyrics?	Students are reading the text too literally. Do they understand tone? How do authors show the "inside" of characters by what they say and do?
Some students aren't annotating throughout the entire passage. Why?		Who is Dan Cody, and what is his significance to Gatsby?	Authors do everything for a reason. Students can ask a question if a part doesn't make sense instead of saying, "This is stupid."
		Gatsby has fantasized about meeting Daisy for so long that she can't possibly meet his dreams.	
		Ewing is Klipspringer's first name, but students don't know who Klipspringer is.	

piece of text that they will assign to their students. Then I ask them to do a think-aloud. During the interview, I instruct each teacher to read a portion of the text out loud, stopping occasionally to tell me what they are thinking. As quickly as I can, I script what each teacher says, trying to capture strategies they use that they might not even be aware of. I will then look for patterns of thinking that they use automatically, which might serve as reading strategies they can model for their students. After my colleague completes the think-aloud, I reread what I scripted and try to synthesize how these expert readers constructed meaning. Following is an example of how Lynn, an International Baccalaureate science teacher, read her college-level biology textbook.

Lynn's patterns of thinking while reading the biology textbook:

- Read text in small chunks.
- Paraphrased each small chunk (explained what the written text meant to her).
- Examined graphics and pinpointed confusion so she could pay close attention to the text as she searched for more information.
- Trusted that the pages of written text would explain the graphics. Read with the intention of connecting the two.
- Categorized information in her head and then on paper so she could refer to it later.
- Reread with a purpose in mind—usually it was to answer a question or clarify a process.

Lynn talked back to her content using language specific to her discipline. It enabled her to determine what was important. This pattern was the same for all of the teachers I interviewed.

At the end of each interview, I asked, "If you had time to teach your students only one thing about the way you read, what would you tell them?"

Lynn, the IB science teacher, said she would ask students, "What story do the diagrams tell?"

Joe, an AP history teacher, said, "History is all about cause and effect."

Barbi, an IB English teacher, said, "The brilliance is in the question."

Kevin, who teaches accounting, said, "Readers have to audit their understanding. They need to ask themselves, what does the information mean to you?"

From each teacher's response, I created a one-page annotation sheet that I could give to students when I went into their content classrooms to do literacy demonstration lessons. I explained to students that each sheet contained suggestions from very good readers, but that they didn't represent the *only* way to read content-specific text. The annotation ideas are a model of how one expert reader talks back to disciplinary text. It is exciting to think how powerful it would be if every teacher shared with his or her students how they annotate content. If each teacher did this, schools couldn't help but grow sophisticated readers of all text structures.

In a science class:

"What story do the diagrams tell?"

Lynn Bruskivage

Recording thinking while reading helps readers remember what they have read. It also provides an opportunity for each reader to wrestle with meaning. Knowing what to write when annotating gives readers a purpose and also helps them determine what is important. Below are some options for annotation:

- Study the *Diagrams* and *Data*. What is significant? What is surprising and what is expected? How does the graphic work? What processes are unclear, and what questions can be asked about the information?

- Record the *What*. Describe what is significant about the process and what conditions make the event possible.

- Record an *Analogy*. Compare the reading to something that is already understood (e.g., lines of military defense to the lines of the immune system's defense).

- Record the *Where*. Where in the body or in nature is the action happening? Are there other places where similar events take place?

- Record questions.

- Record connections to known information.

- Record hypotheses.

- Record thinking that is new or surprising.

In a social studies class:

"It's all about cause and effect."

Joe Colacioppo

Recording thinking while reading helps readers remember what they have read. It also provides an opportunity for each reader to wrestle with meaning. Knowing what to write when annotating gives readers a purpose and also helps them determine what is important. Below are some options for annotation:

- Record the *Who*. Define who the "biggies" in the selection are and why they are important. Consider their political affiliation, special interests, and with whom they align.

- Record the *What*. Describe what is significant about the event and what conditions made the event possible.

- Record the *Why*. Think about why the event is studied and how it affects events and people today.

- Record the *When*. Pinpoint when the event occurred and consider when the issue(s) concerning the event will resurface.

- Record the *Where*. Where in the world is this happening? Is the geography significant, and have other important events happened here before?

- Record connections.

- Record questions.

- Record opinions.

- Record thinking that is new to you.

In a literature class:

"The brilliance is in the question."

Barbi Bess

Recording thinking while reading helps readers remember what they have read. It also provides an opportunity for each reader to wrestle with meaning. Knowing what to write when annotating gives readers a purpose and also helps them determine what is important. Below are some options for annotation:

- Record the *Action*. What is happening in the story? Who is involved in the conflict? Has anyone changed as a result of the struggle?

- Record the **Who**. Identify the protagonist and the antagonist. Examine how other characters fit into the plot. What purposes do they serve?

- Record the *Literary Elements*. Choose a literary element and consider how the author is using it to convey meaning.

- Record the **Where** and **When**. Setting gives the story context. It helps readers know why characters respond the way they do.

- Record anything you notice about the *Author's Craft*. What meaning might the author be trying to convey?

- Record connections to other texts and personal experiences.

- Record questions.

- Record opinions.

- Record your response. What emotions does the work evoke? What can you infer about the author's intent from your response?

In an accounting class:

"Audit your understanding. What does the information mean to you?"

Kevin Van Wormer

Recording thinking while reading helps readers remember what they have read. It also provides an opportunity for each reader to wrestle with meaning. Knowing what to write when annotating gives readers a purpose and also helps them determine what is important. Below are some options for annotation:

- Study the T-charts. Identify the transaction. What is counted as income and what is counted as a debt? How does what you read compare with the visuals in the text?

- Ask questions. What is surprising and what is expected? How does the information affect the client's account? What entries are unclear, and what questions can be asked about the information you have?

- Identify a purpose for digging back into the numbers and text. What do you need to find? What pieces of the accounting puzzle are you missing?

- Mark places that seem confusing. Try to frame confusion by asking a question. Record inconsistencies. What seems out of order?

What Data Do You Trust?

When I was in high school, we would often read the assigned novel or play as a class. The teacher would read aloud while the students were expected to follow along. Occasionally someone in the class would react. Sometimes a student would ask a question or make a connection. The teacher would stop and interact with that student to quell the reaction, answer the question, or give the class information, whether everyone needed it or not. The teacher would then continue reading aloud where she'd left off. By that time, I had checked out.

Annotating can take the place of that whole-class read-aloud that many of us experienced as adolescents. When we ask our students to annotate thinking, we give every one of them an opportunity to think, not just a few of them. In return, we get loads of assessment data that has the power to inform our instruction and improve students' achievement.

I am a skeptic. I distrust outsiders who barge into my classroom, data in hand, making judgments about students they've never met. When data from the district and state level doesn't jibe with what I know about my students, I am driven into a state of cognitive dissonance, often trying to rationalize why the learners in my class didn't do as well as I think they should have. Teachers often experience a state of cognitive dissonance when asked to examine data they don't trust. Some react with anger or denial. When teachers don't trust the data, they don't use it to inform instruction or enhance student performance.

As a teacher I must ask myself, *What data do I trust?* Results from formative assessments push me to change my practice more than a row of numbers does. However, ignoring the summative data that districts collect and compile is not an option. Teachers can't solely rely on the information they receive from outside sources because it doesn't give a complete picture of who our students are. For this reason, I have to have other sources of information that help me improve my instruction. This is where formative assessments become so valuable.

To be the best we can be, teachers must ask themselves, How does the data we are given compare with what we know about our students? If we don't completely trust what we see, we must work hard to collect our own data—data that we trust. Data that I trust is anything that shows me what my students are thinking and learning in real time. Annotated text and sticky notes are quick and easy ways for students to demonstrate what they understand on a regular basis. Annotating gives students multiple ways to show thinking and provides teachers with an opportunity to see how student thinking evolves. Collected over time, annotations are the perfect progress-monitoring tools! In addition to seeing how student thinking grows, teachers can quickly analyze sticky notes and annotations to target specific needs. Mini-lessons are most effective when they come from the students' thinking. Paying close attention to what they write helps teachers provide useful feedback along the way so their students' thinking continues to progress. No data is better than that.

What Works

Assessment Point: Effective assessors remind themselves of what it was like to read something for the first time. They think about what they need to make sense of the text, and they model those strategies for students. They don't waste time teaching strategies or asking students to do tasks that aren't used in the world outside of school. They remember that during the first read, they had to work hard to construct meaning.

Assessment Point: Effective assessors plan their day so students have time to work and create evidence of learning. They decide what tracks of thinking are important for students to leave. They reflect on that evidence to plan the following day's lesson. Effective assessors are always asking themselves, How will students show me their thinking so I can be a better teacher tomorrow?

"Are You Up for a Challenge?"

1. Select a text or type of text that you need your students to be able to read. Carefully think through how you would construct meaning if you were to encounter this particular text structure for the first time. Try annotating something yourself and see if there are certain skills, strategies, or content that you want to highlight for your students. Decide how students will hold their thinking. Will you need to make copies for them to write on or can they use sticky notes?

2. Read student annotations frequently to help you figure out what instruction students need *most* tomorrow. Use their annotations as an instructional point to build future mini-lessons.

CHAPTER 6

Feedback That Fortifies

Feedback that fortifies is a critical part of useful formative assessment. It comes at a time when the learner needs it most to improve performance or product. In the most pragmatic way, feedback helps students find their way back to the process of learning.

—Lorna Earl (2003)

Writing back to students' annotations is one way I give feedback to learners. Another is conferring during work time. This foundational practice—talking to my students one-on-one—is another way I figure out what they understand and what they need next.

Conferring to Give Feedback

Conferring with students during work time is a great way to give them real-time feedback. The trick is taking a few minutes to notice what they need. Before I can give useful feedback, I first must listen to what they have to say about the work they are doing. Conferring is a talent that can take years to develop. Don't get discouraged, though. To kids, even a teacher who confers badly is better than one who doesn't do it at all. There are lots of useful resources on how to improve the way teachers confer. One of the best ways to improve is to just dive in and start trying it. However, watching a skilled colleague confer, and noticing how he or she does it, is not only informative but almost magical.

The Don of Conferring

Twenty-nine years ago, during my student teaching, I observed Donald Graves running a writer's workshop with a group of third graders. Don was a researcher, a university professor, and a writer dedicated to improving the way children learned to write. I remember watching him from the back row, thinking to myself, *Someday, I want to teach like that guy.*

I was struck by the way Don listened to his young readers and writers. They did most of the talking. When Don did talk, his words were short and sweet. Because he listened carefully, he was able to give targeted feedback that offered different ways to dig back into the task. When it came to conferring, Don was the best. Not because he knew the perfect thing to say but because he gave real-time feedback that energized the learner. At the time, I didn't know how much he would influence me as a teacher.

When I confer with students, I try to remember what I learned from Don. My job is not to take over and do the work for them. My job is to find an entry point so that I can give students useful feedback that will encourage them to dive back into the work.

Students need feedback to dig back into their reading as well, so I need to look at student work every day to keep the learning going. Sometimes it takes only a few minutes at the beginning of class to help a student. For example, last night, I read the class's exit tickets. I can tell from what Carlos has written that he has the main characters in *Of Mice and Men* confused. I need to clear up his confusion as fast as possible so that he can keep the story straight. As soon as Carlos enters the room the next morning, I say, "Carlos, in the novel we are reading, George is the smaller, smart guy, and Lennie is the large, strong one who isn't so smart. Write that on a sticky note so you can keep the two characters straight." I hadn't spent valuable minutes responding to exit tickets the night before. Instead I had quickly checked for patterns of understanding and for outliers such as Carlos whose misunderstandings might interfere with the next day's work. One quick conversation is sometimes all it takes to support a student's ability to continue working on his or her own. Knowing that time is limited, I look for minutes I can steal throughout the period to give students real-time feedback.

Other times, a more in-depth conversation has to happen. Conferring during the work time is the perfect opportunity to give students one-on-one support. I can assess understanding and immediately give real-time feedback. Sometimes feedback comes in the form of modeling strategies on how to improve the work. Other times it is responding to the work that is produced or suggesting options for how to proceed.

Anyone can confer, especially if the motive is to support the learner in the learning process. However, some secondary teachers are hesitant to confer because they were never taught how. They often comment that they aren't sure what to do in a conference. Do they let the kids talk about their work and the process? Do they show them different ways to fix the problem? Do they model? My answer is always "Yes!" I suggest that teachers do all of these things. But before they decide which one to do, they must listen to the student and let him or her be the guide. Asking, "How's it going?" is a good starter. When I need direction on how to improve the way I confer, I go to the experts. Patrick Allen's book *Conferring: The Keystone of Reader's Workshop* (2009), and Carl Anderson's *How's It Going? A Practical Guide to Conferring with Student Writers* (2000) are both useful resources for teachers who want to improve in this area.

Go Ahead, Confer. It's Good for Them.

Students reap the benefits of assessment when teachers carefully attend to the results and then take the time to provide useful feedback. Conferring during the work time is an opportune moment to assess and give feedback. However, conferring is a lot more than simply monitoring the room. Sometimes teachers are hesitant to interrupt a student who is busily working. Instead of digging in to assess and enhance understanding of what students are doing, they peek over their shoulders and then move on to the next kid. Unfortunately when teachers do this, they miss out on an ideal opportunity to differentiate instruction. Sometimes, peeking over shoulders to look at student work is a form of assessment. However, assessment alone will not improve achievement. Students also need targeted feedback to improve. When I am deciding how to support learners during a conference, I consider what they might need. Do they need me as a sounding board, or do I need to show them another way to approach the learning? Only with descriptive feedback and an opportunity to rework the learning can my conferring improve a student's performance.

Once the work time starts, it is sometimes hard to know where to go first. Before going anywhere, I scan the room and notice who is reading and who is stuck. Today I see Vinnie randomly digging through his backpack. After a few seconds he starts to stare off into space. Next, he looks around the room to see what his friend Max is doing. He tries to get Max's attention but can't, because Max is engrossed in his reading. I head over to Vinnie, guessing that he needs a nudge to get going. Vinnie spots me heading his way and quickly pulls out his book. I pull a chair up to his desk and ask, "So, Vinnie, what did you write on your sticky notes last class period?" Without saying a word, Vinnie turns his book so I can read what they say. I turn the book back to him and ask him to tell me which one he cares about the most.

Vinnie is reading Sherman Alexie's *The Absolutely True Diary of a Part-Time Indian*. He reads the sticky note he cares about and then asks, "How come, in every book that we read, the main character has a problem?" Right off the bat, Vinnie's question gives me an entry point. I can tell that he isn't connecting what he knows about story structure to this novel.

"Oh wow," I say. "I was just talking to Max before class about this. I can tell you guys are friends. You think a lot alike. Max wanted to know why every novel he reads in school is depressing. I told him that a lot of novels are depressing because of the problem introduced at the beginning of the book. The problem often gets the story started. Then there are events that occur that lead to some kind of resolution. A resolution doesn't mean that everything is worked out. It just means that the problem has been addressed. Often the main character has changed in some way." Vinnie nods but doesn't look at me, so I push a little more. "What would you say is the problem that gets this story started?"

Vinnie looks up at me but doesn't say anything. I wait. After a bit he says, "Probably that Arnold wants to get an education and if he stays on the rez, he won't get a very good one."

"Right. So what happens when he decides to leave the reservation and go to the white school many miles away?"

"More problems for Arnold."

"Right. Can you name a few?"

"I'm not sure."

"Okay, here's what I want you to do today. As you read, I want you to pay attention to the problems that Arnold encounters. I also want you to see how each problem is addressed. Look for changes in Arnold after these events occur. Maybe his attitude will be different, or maybe he'll get smarter about how to deal with kids at his new school or the kids on the 'rez.'" Vinnie starts digging in his backpack for a pencil, so I'm not sure if he knows what I want him to do. I ask him, "Can you tell me back what I want you to look for?"

Vinnie stops digging and says, "Yeah, I'm gonna see if Arnold learns anything from all the bad things that keep happening to him."

"Terrific," I say. "How will you hold your thinking so that during the debriefing you can share what you've figured out with your group?"

"I think after each problem, I can write a sticky note about the way Arnold changes."

A Note About Texts

The class anchor text is Sherman Alexie's *The Absolutely True Diary of a Part-Time Indian*. In addition to reading the novel, I provide choice by locating several companion pieces that are mainly short, nonfiction excerpts or articles. I look for high-interest texts so that readers of all levels will want to work to read something every day. Companion pieces that I collect are intended to build background knowledge and give the reader historical context for the novel.

I recognize that when the entire class is reading the same book, I am not meeting everyone's needs. Therefore, I provide choice in the companion pieces that I select. I look for ones that range in difficulty and length so that each day students can choose one that fits their needs. Using *The Absolutely True Diary of a Part-Time Indian* affords me the opportunity to teach the whole class certain mini-lessons while the companion pieces give readers choice and the opportunity to build background knowledge, improve fluency, and increase vocabulary.

When the class anchor text is too difficult for some readers, I have to make some modifications that will allow them access to text of the same quality as the rest of the class is getting to read and discuss. One modification is to download the text onto a listening device. This allows the readers who are struggling or falling behind to listen while they read and still participate in the work time and the discussion that takes place during the debriefing.

I have discovered that students aren't embarrassed to use the listening modifications. Many are willing to load the book onto their own listening device once I explain to them that I don't consider it cheating. I have written a few grants to buy devices for kids who don't have one. Before we start the novel, I download the text so that as soon as I realize someone is struggling to keep up, I can give them a device. Often they use the listening device to get interested in the book or caught up with the rest of the class.

It is a matter of equity that all students have an opportunity to be exposed to high-quality text. Too often struggling readers get left out of juicy conversations because they have been unable to keep up with the class reading. Some resort to cheating. Others just quit. However, struggling readers also need an opportunity every day to read and construct meaning on their own. For this reason, I work hard to find companion pieces that are accessible and interesting so all readers can practice comprehending text every day.

"Great. I'll count on you to get your discussion group started by sharing what you figured out. So be ready to share what you noticed in about twenty minutes."

When I confer with students, I keep a few objectives in mind so that my feedback is as targeted as possible. During a conference, I listen to see what readers understand. I ask myself three questions:

- What does this student need right now to keep reading and writing?
- How can I help the student get smarter about the content or be more strategic about the process?
- What will I ask the student to do when I leave?

Keeping these three questions in mind, I zigzag across the room and head to Jade. Even though she has improved a great deal over the course of the year, she struggles when it comes to reading for extended periods of time. Short spurts of regular feedback help her to reenter the reading and writing when she gets tired or confused. Because I've listened in on her discussion group, I've learned that Jade doesn't have a lot of confidence that she is making sense of text. When doubt sets in, she stops trying and waits for someone to tell her what the reading is about. Often her good buddy Sammi is the one who does this for her. Unfortunately, Sammi isn't always sure what is happening either.

I pull a chair next to Jade and ask her to find an annotation that she thinks is pretty good. It doesn't take her long to choose, because she has only one. While Jade rereads her sticky, I pull out my notebook that I've set up for this class. I turn to the pages I've delineated for Jade.

I show Jade her page. It reads, "Jade quits reading too quickly. Find out why. Does she understand what she is reading? What causes her to quit? Help her build *endurance*."

Jade reads what I have written, half to herself and half aloud. She finishes reading and looks at me. "So," I ask, "what do you think about what I wrote?"

Sheepishly, Jade smiles and looks at her desk. "I quit when I get stuck."

I look at her for a minute. I'm not sure what to say to her, because for the last six months we have been working on strategies to repair meaning, and Jade is still quitting. "Okay," I say. "Let's read what you wrote on your sticky."

Jade reads aloud, "Why doesn't Arnold have anything to be thankful for? Can't he be thankful about his family and friends and stuff? That's what I do."

"What made you decide to write this?" I ask.

"I don't get this part." Jade points to the line that is causing her confusion. I ask her to read it aloud. She reads, "Arnold said, 'At least they didn't kill all the Indians.'" Jade cracks a smile.

"That's funny to you?"

"Yeah," she says. "His life is so bad that he is thankful that the white people didn't kill all the Indians. He's Indian. Don't you get why that's funny?"

"Yeah, I think so. Why do you think it's funny?" I ask, even though I can tell she has picked up the narrator's satire. I want her to describe the literary device so she can recognize it again. I also want Jade to explain what she knows to prove to herself that she understands her reading a lot better than she gives herself credit for.

"Arnold is really sarcastic. It's funny in a sad way that that is all he has to be thankful for. He is thankful for something that shouldn't even have happened. The whites didn't kill all the Indians, but they put them on reservations, which was almost as bad."

"Right—you totally get this part," I say excitedly. "Okay, so now you have to mark this place with something so you can share it with your group. Sammi will love this part. She will think it is pretty cool that you are sharing something funny with her."

Jade starts to write a note on her sticky. She strategically places it by the line so that she can read it to her group and then share her thinking. Before I leave Jade, I want her to be clear that she needs to keep reading and writing, so I ask her if she is up for a challenge. She tells me she is, so I say, "Okay, as you read today, I want you to look for a couple more places where Arnold is being funny in a sad kind of way. You are right on target with his sarcastic sense of humor. See if you find some more places where he is using humor to cover up his pain. Mark them with sticky notes and then write a few thoughts down so you remember what you were thinking." Before I have finished, I see that Jade has already started reading. It's time for me to be quiet and let her get to work. It dawns on me that Jade doesn't trust herself as a reader because her state test scores have told her for years that she is not a good reader. She trusts her scores more than she trusts herself. Before I forget, I jot myself a note: "Once a week, have Jade lead her group. Continue to help her name what she comprehends."

The Teaching and Learning Cycle Begins with Assessment

I used to believe that the cycle of teaching and learning always started with the teaching part. I've revised my thinking on this. I realize now that unless I start with a little assessing, I'm teaching in a vacuum. If I give students a way to show me what they understand first, I have a way to see what they know so I can better gauge what they need.

Think back to the workshop model described in Chapter 3. As you read the following paragraphs, notice the different opportunities I have to give students feedback.

In addition to sharing the learning targets during the **opening** of workshop, I often give the class a short task that serves as a pre-assessment. Sometimes, these pre-assessments are a quick response to a quote written on the board. Other times, students are instructed to brainstorm on a sticky note what they know about a certain topic. If they don't know anything, they are asked to write a question that will help me give them some background knowledge on the topic. Pre-assessments during the opening help me to know if the mini-lesson I've planned consists of too much or not enough information. I'm working toward the "Goldilocks" principle: How much information is "just right" to help students dig into the work time?

During the mini-lesson, I teach a specific skill, strategy, or piece of content based on student learning from the day before. Once the **mini-lesson** is finished, students are released to work on something that will show me how well they have understood the learning that was just introduced. While they are working, I have another chance to assess. Now, I can confer and give feedback that will help students dig deeper into content. As I help individuals, I am also looking for class patterns of confusion that will inform what I teach in the mini-lesson the following day.

During the **debriefing**, students leave me some sort of written work (inner-voice sheet, sticky note, response, etc.) that is evidence of their thinking for that day. From there I can give feedback by conferring with them the next day or writing comments that I attach to their work. If the feedback is useful, students are inclined to use it to rework or improve whatever it is they are learning. When time is built in for students to apply the feedback, they get smarter.

Feedback needs to be targeted throughout the teaching and learning cycle because it directs kids back to learning. Without time to apply the feedback, lengthy comments and conferences are a waste of time. If I wait and give feedback only when an assignment is due, the feedback is too late to be useful. Feedback at the end of a unit of study is summative in nature and can only judge, rank, or sort student performance. By the time final drafts, projects, and tests are due, students should have had several learning opportunities to grow and improve. If they've had these opportunities, both teachers and students are confident that they have done their best. Current learning can be fairly measured, and the class can move on to the next learning goal. When teachers have the belief that one is never finished learning, they can look their students in the eye and say, "This is where you are now at this particular point in time with this particular piece of learning. If you don't quit, you'll continue to get smarter."

"I Can't Get to Every Kid Every Day!"

Neither can I. I feel successful when I can confer with everyone once every two weeks. I have to use the debriefing time of workshop as another way to touch base with and give feedback to the students with whom I haven't recently conferred. Below is an example of how I use the entire workshop to assess and give feedback.

It is close to the end of the year, and students in my reading workshop class are reading self-selected texts. I want them to reflect on my yearlong goal for them: knowing that books can change their lives. I also want to hear what they think about how reading can give them experiences that they otherwise would not have. As one of our final lessons, I model how the book I am currently reading has influenced my thinking.

Mini-lesson: *Books help us see another person's perspective. I model how the book I am reading gives me insight into a life I wouldn't otherwise know about.*

I begin the mini-lesson by saying, "I am reading *Gang Leader for a Day* by Sudkir Venkatesh. This book is about a sociology student who infiltrates a Chicago gang in hopes of discovering how the inner circle of gangs works. I am learning why some kids in poverty turn to gangs." I put a few paragraphs from a key chapter under the document camera and read them aloud, pausing to annotate and share my thinking. I add, "This book is changing me as a reader because I am getting to see gang life through the eyes of a sociologist who faces some really intense challenges. I need to keep reading because I want to find out if there is a way for people to escape this pattern of violence." I instruct students that their job today is to think about the way their book is changing them.

Work time: While the students read, I move around the room looking for someone to confer with. I will ask them to share with me how they are using the mini-lesson as a purpose for today's reading. I don't get to everyone, so when the work time is drawing to a close, I ask students to grab a sticky note and jot down how the book has given them insight into something new.

Debriefing: A few students have a chance to share what they wrote before the bell rings. I close class by saying, "I can't wait to see what the rest of you wrote.

I'll use what you figured out today to see how we can go even deeper into our texts tomorrow."

As I plan for the following day, I look at the sticky notes that students wrote during the debriefing to learn about their thinking and prioritize whom to meet with first during the next class period. I decide to meet with Dre, Sarah, Erik, and Flora, based on their comments and the fact that it's been at least a week since I've checked in with them.

Dre writes on his sticky note, "I feel good about myself. I actually found a book I can sit down and read. I'm confused because I don't know what *incarcerated* means." Dre is reading *Inside the Crips* by Colton Simpson.

I decide to grab Dre as he walks into the room the next day. I ask him to get out his book and show me where he got stuck during the previous class. He reads aloud a short paragraph. Dre struggles to pronounce *incarceration*. The word keeps appearing in his book. When I pronounce the word for him, he immediately says, "I know what that word is. It means being locked up. I get it now." *Incarceration* was a word he knew from his background knowledge but had never seen in print. Once I pronounced it for him, I knew he would be able to read on his own during the work time.

Sarah's comment requires a little more time to address than Dre's. I will have to meet with her in a conference during work time. She wrote, "This book makes me think about how bad life must be for a kid who lives with an alcoholic. I don't understand why Dave never told anyone he was being abused." Sarah is reading *A Child Called It* by Dave Peltzer.

I tell Sarah that once we start reading, I will come by to confer with her first. Instead of trying to answer her question, I reread it and praise her for asking one without an easy answer. Then I throw out a question of my own. "Great question. It seems suspicious to me too that none of the teachers at Dave's school noticed he had been stabbed. I wonder if the author is exaggerating." I ask her if she knows the book *A Million Little Pieces* by James Frey.

Sarah shakes her head and says, "No."

I decide to give her some background knowledge about the author and teach her about unreliable narrators. I explain how James Frey duped Oprah when he appeared on her show and claimed that his book was autobiographical, when in fact many parts had been embellished. Later the author admitted that his book had some fictional elements. I want to make Sarah more skeptical of what she reads instead of taking everything at face value. I challenge her to look for more examples of possibly embellished text. I leave Sarah and head over to Erik. The comment written on his sticky note made me curious. Erik wrote, "I'm not really confused about anything today. I feel different though. My thinking has changed. I'm more open-minded about addictions. I used to think people used addiction as an excuse to get wasted." Erik is reading *Go Ask Alice* by an anonymous author.

I ask Erik to explain what he meant. He tells me that until he read *Go Ask Alice*, he thought that people who used drugs just said they were addicts because they wanted to party. "It seems that addiction is a sickness and not just an excuse." Erik goes on to tell me about a family member who abuses drugs and how he has been angry with her. She says she uses drugs because she is an addict. I let Erik talk and make connections between the book and his life. Today, my job is to listen and be his sounding board. I let the novel do the teaching. I thank him for his thinking and move on to Flora.

Flora is also making personal connections between her book and her very difficult life. She wrote on her sticky note, "Seeing a girl gang member reminds me of my cousin's world. I understand better why she chose to be in a gang." Flora is reading *Lady Q: The Rise and Fall of a Latin Queen* by Sonia Rodriguez and Reymundo Sanchez. I pull up a chair next to Flora and ask her to tell me how she has gotten smarter as a result of reading this book. Flora says, "My dad is so worried that I will join a gang. Now I know why. I had no idea how bad girl gangs are. I need to tell my dad that he has nothing to worry about. There is no way I'll be in a gang." I look at Flora and hope she can stay true to her word.

Conferring is not a race to see how fast I can fix every kid. I must avoid the urge to rush in and take over for students who are struggling. If I truly want students to get better, I need to use conferring as another venue to respond to their learning. Conferring is one more way that I can support students with feedback so they are able to dig back into the learning process.

Put It in Writing: Another Way to Give Feedback

Conferring isn't the only way to give students real-time feedback. Often I can give it by responding with short written responses to their annotations or comments they've left in other formats. It is important to give students lots of different ways to demonstrate their thinking so that they are aware of what is happening in their heads as they read. Often student thinking is held using the following tools: sticky notes, annotations on a piece of text, anchor charts, inner-voice sheets, group observation forms, double-entry diaries, and response journals. Students don't have to write a lot for me to see what they understand. Because what they write is manageable, I am able to look at it quickly and respond regularly to at least some of the thinking they leave for me. Initially, students are surprised that I read what they write. Sometimes I find strange comments they have left for me, hoping to confirm their suspicion that I don't read what they have written. When I respond, some realize that they will be held accountable for how they read and what they write. Most important, they start to understand that their thinking matters.

In the first week of school, I start students off slowly, asking them to practice showing me their thinking on short, high-interest pieces of text. Very quickly I crank up the difficulty of the reading and the task by asking them to show me how they are thinking with longer, more complex reading.

The following examples come from a three-page excerpt from one of Joy Hakim's books in The History of US series. The juniors in my eleventh-grade American Literature class are reading *The Great Gatsby*. It will be important for them to know a little bit about the 1920s so they will have context for the characters' actions. I frequently use Hakim's books because they are accessible and informative. Students will find it challenging to read the 1920s excerpt not because the words are too hard but because they have little background knowledge about the time period and little interest in learning more about it. When they read text they don't care about, often they get bored and their minds begin to wander. I decide that my mini-lesson for the day needs to show students how to better monitor their comprehension. If they can help themselves interact with the text before they've read too far thinking of something else, they will be better readers of all text.

I have several learning targets or goals for the day. I want students to practice monitoring their comprehension so they'll know when their minds start to wander. I want them to try to consciously apply one of the strategies I model in the mini-lesson to get themselves reengaged with the text. Last, I want students to build background knowledge about the 1920s so they have context for the class anchor text.

Mini-lesson: *Good readers recognize how to use inner voice to monitor their comprehension.* I take an excerpt from one of the companion pieces that students will eventually choose. I model how I listen to the thinking in my head and try to decide if it is interacting with ideas on the page or wandering from the text. I record how I think on the document camera so kids can see how I am annotating. I model how I ask questions to isolate confusion. I show the class how I make connections between the text and what I know about the world. I write a few reactions to new information and then release students to try it on their own.

Work time:　Students read and annotate. I confer. I catch the class when I hear thinking that the rest of the class can benefit from.

Debriefing:　I ask a few students to share what they figured out about the 1920s and request that they leave their annotated articles, so that I can see tracks of their thinking to decide where we'll go tomorrow.

That afternoon, I read each annotation and give at least three pieces of feedback to each student. The feedback is still short, but in addition to praising their thinking, I want to improve the way they respond to text. I also want to see how they've monitored their comprehension and grown in their knowledge of the 1920s.

As I read what students have written, I quickly count the number of annotations—I have challenged them at the beginning of class to give me at least three pieces of thinking per page. Nine annotations written throughout the selection will give me a lot of information about their abilities to comprehend and interact with text over an extended period of time. I can learn a lot about my students, and I won't have to write a lot back to them if I keep the following three tasks in mind:

- Comment on something the student did well.
- Teach the student something about the content or how to read more strategically.
- Identify for myself what the student will need tomorrow to continue working independently.

As I dig into their written responses, I notice José's paper is on top. He is quiet and rarely talks in class. When he does, his voice is soft, and his thick accent sometimes makes it difficult for me to understand him. José's first annotation connects "fad contests" (like the dance step the Charleston) of the 1920s to today's *American Idol* and *America's Best Dance Crew*. I praise his connection and remind him of our yearlong guiding question, What makes Americans unique? by writing a quick note next to his annotation: "I wonder if being highly competitive is something unique to Americans. What do you think?"

I read on and see that José is struck by the picture of and caption about women being arrested, dressed in flapper garb. He writes, "I am surprised they resisted getting arrested. I have never seen people do that." I write back, "Let's Google some images tomorrow. I bet we can find other pictures of Americans resisting arrest."

On the second page, José highlights the part in the text that describes the anti-immigration sentiments of the 1920s. He hasn't written anything in the margins, so I am curious to know what he thinks. Next to the highlighted text, I write, "Why did you decide to highlight these lines?" I turn the page and see that José has asked a question. "What war happened right before the 1920s? World War I or II?" I jot down "WWI."

José has more annotations than the nine I asked for. I give him feedback on only four. However, I read them all and learn that he reads faster and comprehends better than I thought. I make a note in my conferring notebook to guide him toward more sophisticated text. Tomorrow, I will show him some pictures of others who have bucked the system. Letting him read about bootleggers and suffragists will be the perfect place for him to start the next class. At the top of José's paper, I write "9/9" (one point for each annotation I required) and the comment, "I am so glad that you know how to annotate. You are quiet in class, so it is good that you can show me your thinking through writing."

Next, I grab Shanice's paper. Flipping through it, I see writing only on the first page. She has written three comments and left the other two pages blank. Her first annotation reads, "dancing too much, t.v. maker, getting in trouble for what?" Shanice is a good reader. I've given her a few novels from the Around the Way Girls series (multiple authors) that she has devoured. She complains during class that she doesn't like to read history. She was off task a lot during the work time, but I am still surprised that she wrote so little. The text should have been easier for her and, in my opinion, pretty interesting. I am not sure how to guide her thinking because she wrote so little. Refusing to show her thinking isn't an option. Without it, I can't tailor instruction to meet her needs. At the top of her paper I mark "3/9." Below the points I write, "I have a feeling you have a lot more thinking than you are showing. Tomorrow during work time, please find a quiet spot and see if you can dig into the reading. If you can show me what you know and wonder through your annotations, I can do a better job finding you interesting text." I am honest with Shanice in my comments, but I know she will need more than a few words written at the top of her paper. Tomorrow I will meet with her first to figure out why she isn't working. I will check to see if she knows how to annotate. I will show her how I annotated the text and make sure she has a quiet place to work. Lastly, I will give her a choice of two different texts that she can choose to read.

My main goal when giving feedback is to help students dive back into the work so they can practice reading, writing, and thinking more independently and strategically. I move through the pile of annotated text quickly. I pick up Katie's. She has written several annotations that have to do with vocabulary and unknown words: "What is a *bootlegger*? What does *ironic* mean? What does *desperate times* mean?"

On her paper, I explain what a bootlegger is. Next to the word *desperate*, I write, "difficult, very hard." In my written comment, I prompt her to jot down some additional thinking by suggesting that she highlight only the unknown words so she can ask questions about the time period. I encourage her to go deeper by writing, "Pick one or two terms you are curious about and see if you can ask a bigger question about the idea that connects to the unknown word." Then I write a question so she can see what I mean. The next day she shows me the question she has asked: "Were bootleggers in the 1920s as dangerous as drug dealers are today?" Thanks to the little bit of feedback, she was able to reenter the task and demonstrate a higher level of thought.

I move on to Kai. She is a good student who always does more than I assign. She is quiet like José. Without tracks of her thinking in writing, I would have a hard time knowing what she understands. I read her first page of annotations. Almost all of them are superficial comments. She has written, "The 1920s must have been hard." She makes a connection: "The dance contests then were like *Dancing with the Stars* today." I go through each page, but nothing she has written indicates to me that she is getting any smarter about the time period. I try to push her by using some written feedback to see if I can get her to make some connections between the 1920s and today. In the margins on the first page I write, "How were the economic conditions of the 1920s similar to what people are experiencing today?" I also write, "Why do you think I am having the class build background about the 1920s before we read *The Great Gatsby*? How will knowing about the time period help you relate to the characters of the book?" Throwing out a few questions will set a purpose for the reading Kai will do tomorrow. Instead of just reading and retelling what she read, I'm hoping that my nudge will get her to go beyond the facts and make some comparisons and contrasts.

When I turn to the second page, I notice that Kai has underlined the words *materialistic age*. In the margin she writes, "meaning: money, cars, clothes, jewels, pretty much fancy things."

Below her writing, I write, "Yes!" simply confirming her definition.

On the next section of text, Kai highlights the words, "There were growing numbers of unemployed people." Next to the highlighted parts, she writes, "So is this the time when the bad economy came into play?" Below what she has written I write, "What do you mean by came into play? Can you give me some examples of what makes a bad economy?"

When I respond to students' thinking by asking questions, my intent is to encourage them to go beyond the literal or factual level of the text. When Shaq asks, "During the 1920s, why did some people try to prevent other people from drinking alcohol?" I don't answer his question. Instead I write, "Why do some people today want to prevent other people from smoking marijuana?"

When kids ask *how* or *why* questions, they are usually too complex for me to answer with a quick written response. I don't feel compelled to answer them at this particular time. I would rather empower students to find answers to their own questions so they don't always rely on me. For this reason, I try to show them different ways they can think about the questions they have. Sometimes I can infer an answer to a question I have asked by making a connection to something I know. The questions that students ask also help me know when I need to bring in more content so they have background knowledge to pull from. Often I try to write questions back to students that encourage them to make their own connections.

There are times when I do answer students' questions. For example, when José asked what war the text was referring to, I wrote "WWI." I try to answer questions that start with *who, what*, or *when*, because the information I give can help students clarify what they are reading. When readers know the *who, what*, or *when*, they can often start asking questions that start with how and why, which are crucial when it comes to developing critical-thinking skills.

Feedback That Drives Student Discussion

After students have spent time reading and writing, it is important for them to synthesize their thinking through talk. When readers have an opportunity to discuss their reading, they often understand it more deeply. Sometimes large-group discussions end up involving only a few students who dominate the conversation while the rest of the class checks out. Having small groups of five or six kids greatly increases the opportunities for more students to have purposeful talk. It also makes them more accountable to their peers. It is a lot harder to hide in a group of six than in a class of thirty-six. Sometimes teachers are hesitant to let kids get into discussion groups because they worry that they'll get off task if the teacher isn't there to monitor every group, every minute.

Figure 6.1

Ways to Help Discussion Groups Function Better

For groups to function well, they need

- something juicy to talk about;
- to have some thinking held so when the group gets off task, a group member can get others on task by sharing a piece of thinking;
- strategies to learn how to take turns and how to politely disagree;
- a purpose; and
- accountability.

In preparation for writing my second book, *Do I Really Have To Teach Reading?* (2004), I studied all different kinds of groups to see what systems and structures were in place when conversations were effective and productive. In Chapter 7 of that text, I share several ideas that have made my group work more effective. In Figure 6.1, I've jotted down a few reminders that help me get the most from small-group discussions. Students discuss longer and more fruitfully when they write first. When their thinking is held in their books, on inner-voice sheets, in double-entry diaries, or on sticky notes before they come together to talk, they are more apt to stay on topic.

Small-group discussions often take place during the debriefing time of workshop. They are another great opportunity for me to assess student understanding. Sometimes I give feedback directly to the discussion group. Other times, I use what I hear to help me plan for the next class. The group observation form from *Do I Really Have to Teach Reading?* helps me record what I see and hear. Initially I used this tool to hold students accountable for productive talk. Little did I know how useful it would be when it came to giving feedback and assessing how students discussed and understood content. The original idea came from former first-grade teacher Colleen Buddy. Colleen used the two-column sheet to keep track of her students' strengths and weaknesses that she noticed during one-on-one conferences. I wanted to use the sheet to keep track of my students' strengths and weaknesses as well. However, I adjusted it so that I could also keep track of what students were learning about the content.

Here's how I adapt Colleen's idea: I collect strengths and weaknesses just like Colleen did, but I add a middle column where I can record smart comments that students say about their reading. I copy several blank sheets and attach them to my clipboard. As students talk, I listen in on their group conversations and record what I see and hear. I categorize what students are doing well and what I need to teach them in upcoming mini-lessons.

When I first started using this sheet, I was the only one privy to the amazing thinking taking place around the room. For years, I tried to figure out how to make the thinking of individual groups public so the entire class could get smarter. In the last several years, the group observation form has morphed into a feedback sheet as well as an assessment tool. Before students leave for the day, I put the completed discussion sheet on the document camera for everyone to see. I point out what went well and use the middle column where I've held students' words to review and emphasize important content.

I can also use the completed group observation form the next time the class gets into groups. It serves as a reminder of what we were working on the last time we discussed. The right-hand and left-hand columns name behaviors and processes observed, as well as ones that need to be taught. The strategies that worked well are listed in the left-hand column. The difficulties that groups experienced are listed in the right-hand column. The middle column holds an abbreviated review of the content discussed. I can use this completed sheet to brainstorm how to negotiate a difficulty or encourage students to continue using a strategy that enabled the group discussion.

Figure 6.2 is an example of a completed group observation form. The students were discussing the novel *1984* by George Orwell. (Keep in mind that real-time feedback is the most useful to students. The sheets I share with the kids are messy rough drafts, not neatly typed rows like the one that follows.)

Before the period ends, I put this sheet on the document camera and share it with the class. I point out what the group did well in terms of discussing, and I share the smart things I heard them say. I make sure I give students credit by name for the processes they do well. During the next class, when it is time to get into discussion groups, I pull out the sheet from the previous class and share the third column, reminding students of some of the behaviors that weren't conducive to group work. This serves as feedback to help them work more productively.

Feedback at the End Is Too Late

When students feel unsuccessful, they quit trying because they don't know what else to do. Several years ago, I saw next to a trash can a graded

Figure 6.2 Group Observation Form

1984, October 15		
+	**Student Quotes**	**General Things We Need to Work On**
Most students had their books with sticky notes holding their thinking.		Students who hadn't read or held their thinking on sticky notes didn't have much to say. They seemed bored. Brainstorm: How can readers who are behind catch up with the group?
Toshay referenced page numbers and grounded her group in the plot before she asked her question.	Toshay: "Does the line that I just read mean that Charrington is part of the thought police?" Juthina: "Wait, who is Charrington?" Toshay: "He's the old guy that runs the antique store."	A group member shared a comment and no one responded. Brainstorm: possible responses.
Joe asked a question and Leon tried to clarify it.	Joe: "Why is Winston being set up? What was O'Brien doing to Winston?" Toshay: "Yeah, does Winston die?" Leon: "Winston is being shocked by O'Brien and we don't know if he dies yet. We have to keep reading."	Kids who didn't have their desks facing each other didn't discuss as well as those who did. Some kids finished with their discussion early. Brainstorm: How does a group know it is finished?
Everyone had a chance to talk.	Javier: "I think that O'Brien is trying to brainwash Winston. It's not good to have people disagree with you if you are trying to oppress them." Andrew: "If people are really busy with just surviving, they don't think about how bad the government is." Kahlia: "Yeah, like today, we are in war, the economy is bad. People are just trying to pay their bills so they don't have time to worry about voting and the government."	Some people who got stuck quit. Brainstorm: What can readers do when they are confused?

Figure 6.3
Discarded Test

HISTORY OF THE MOB

Use complete sentences only. Use ink only.

1. Explain why Colosimo was killed. Colosimo was killed because he refused to expand his prostitution into Alchichol.

2. Explain the three major enemies Capone was faced with in his quest for control of Chicago. The 3 things Capone faced was the police, the Irish Gangs and the Sicilians

3. What happened on Feb. 14, 1929, in Chicago? To what gang? Why? The St. Valintines Day massacer, to the Bugs Moran mob because they were his rivals.

4. In New York City Italians and Jews formed an alliance for profit. Who were they? They were the Masteah Petes, Costello, Lucky

5. What was the Castelle/Marese war? Who was it between? Who won? Why?

social studies test that a student had attempted to throw away (Figure 6.3). Curious, I picked it up and read the questions to see if I could answer any of them. I had trouble focusing on the questions because my eyes kept coming back to the giant *D* circled at the top of the page. The *"What?"* written several times down the middle didn't help, either. Upon further examination, I noticed the large minus ten written where the student had written nothing. In all honesty, the kid had answered more questions than I could have. However, I knew by the way it was graded why the student had thrown it away. Not only were the marks demoralizing, but they were useless in terms of feedback. All they told the student was that he or she hadn't memorized the right facts. In a world of never-ending access to factual information, there is no shame in not remembering trivia—especially when it can be looked up in an instant. The test got thrown away because the learner didn't value the score, or the feedback or letter grade at the top. On the bright side, the owner of the D test had at least had the courtesy to throw it away in someone else's trash can.

The example in Figure 6.3 is a form of written feedback. Unfortunately, this feedback has come too late for this student to get better. Before I rethought how I gave feedback, my students also threw away their graded work. They didn't pitch everything, only some things. How did my students decide what to keep and what to trash? Usually they pitched final essays and quizzes that weren't As or Bs before they even read the comments. Sometimes I'd pass back their work and watch them roll their eyes or mutter unmentionables underneath their breath. When this happened, I would ask myself, *If they hate their grades so much, why don't they try harder?* It wasn't until I started to examine how I gave feedback that I realized my students were sending me the message that my grades and comments came too late for them to care. Letter grades, missed points, and cursory comments written in the margins at the end weren't enough to make students reenter the learning process. When learners are discouraged, they quit. Once learners quit, teachers are in trouble.

This year, I begin my twenty-seventh year of teaching at a new school, and I find myself standing before students who are struggling more than any I've ever taught. At any given time, one can hear forty-one different languages spoken in the halls. The state test scores are low, and the numbers for free and reduced lunch are high. Sitting before me are the achievement gap kids that I have so often read about in the data and professional literature.

After only the second day of class, I notice that at any inkling of impending difficulty or struggle, my students would rather go to the bathroom or wait in long lines to change their schedule than work through it. Avoidance behaviors abound. When struggle sets in, many are overcome with sudden bouts of narcolepsy. Others fish for their phones, searching for friends who have also given up. Their threshold for struggle is low, and I know that if I don't start to build their endurance, I will spend the entire year trying to keep them on task. Many of these students gave up long before they got to me. Some give up because they see no signs of getting better. Others quit to save face. Many just don't know what else to do.

Students need useful feedback, and they need it now. My main job as a teacher is to show learners how to improve. They need lots of time to read and write, but in order for students to stay on task, they need to know what to do when reading and writing gets difficult. When students don't initially understand something, I can't give them a zero or an F. Instead I need to give them specific feedback so that they can go back to their work and reengage in the learning process. Feedback must be timely. If I want students to get better, "do-overs" have to be an option.

When assessment comes only at the end of the teaching and learning cycle, students are often surprised by their grade and translate the feedback they get as criticism. Worse yet, when feedback isn't given along the way, letter grades and percentiles often confirm students' perceptions that they aren't capable of doing better work. Administering summative assessments and assigning final grades don't promote learning and rarely improve achievement. Typically, it only confirms for students that they either get it or they don't—that they are the A, B, or C student they've always been. All students can do better if they are taught along the way how to do better.

What Works

Assessment Point: Effective assessors know that to improve student learning, they have to do more than just measure students' performance. Timely and useful feedback has to accompany the assessment. The feedback can be short, but it must be timely.

Assessment Point: Effective assessors know that feedback comes in a variety of ways. It doesn't have to be drawn out or complicated. Sometimes just a short comment is all the student needs to dig back into the learning process.

"Are You Up for a Challenge?"

1. Brainstorm different ways you give students feedback. If you give feedback only at the end of a unit or on a final piece of writing, think how you might give students insight into how they can improve before the product is due. Don't feel

like you have to give feedback on everything. Instead, set a goal for yourself to increase the incidents of feedback you already do by two.

2. Find times during the class period to steal minutes to talk to kids. A quick conference at the beginning of class and more thoughtful conferences during the work time all add up to powerful minutes of instruction.

CHAPTER 7

Grading Is Killing Me

Happiness is neither virtue nor pleasure nor this thing nor that, but simply growth. We are happy when we are growing.

—*John Butler Yeats (1946)*

Grading. I hate it. As a teacher, it is what I wrestle with most. I know it is one of the necessary evils of the job, but I find myself constantly struggling with issues of management and equity. It's difficult to grade what I can't see or hear, so I'm always wondering if I'm giving students fair ways to show me what they know. Sometimes I go overboard and give kids so many ways to show me their thinking that I get overwhelmed with the grading. Being fair and being able to manage the way I grade is a difficult balancing act.

A large part of this balancing act depends on how I ask students to show me what they know. I must be careful to grade in a way that reflects what students understand and what I value. I have to be careful that my attempts to "stay on top of things" don't sacrifice fairness for the sake of management. Grading in ways that are easy to manage but not fair to the learner or reflective of what I value is something that happens all too often. Case in point: Tate and the science teacher.

Hi Mr. F,

Tate and I were reviewing her grade in your class and noticed that she received a zero in the grade book for the assignment "Kleenex box." As a teacher myself, I know it is expensive to outfit a classroom, and I am happy to provide you with any supplies you need. Tate will bring you a whole pack of Kleenex boxes tomorrow.

Going forward, I would appreciate it if Tate's grade only reflected her understanding of science.

Thanks for all your work in the classroom,

Colleen (Tate's mom)

Grades That Reflect What Students Learn and What Teachers Value

I would bet that Tate's science teacher doesn't value tissues more than his students' knowledge of biology. Yet his grading practice sends a different message. In these tight times, schools have to resort to relying on parents more and more to outfit the classrooms with essentials. There's no student writing attached to this "assignment," which makes giving it points a breeze. Students earn either fifty points or none at all. However, giving points to "reward" students who bring in the supplies shouldn't count as a reflection of what they've learned.

Before I could articulate my grading practices for readers, I had to consider several questions:

- How do I manage the grading of seventy-five or more students?
- How do I prevent students from getting discouraged when their grades are low?
- How do I get and give the best information about student performance in the shortest amount of time?
- How do I make sure that what I am grading reflects what a student knows, can do, and understands over time?

What Do They Really Know?
The Summer Reading Quiz

Students often give us the impetus to change. It's the third day of school. As students file in, I overhear various conversations taking place around the room. Right before the bell rings, I hear Lydia and Brittany announcing to anyone who will listen that in spite of not reading, they aced the summer reading quiz. I'm not the teacher who gave them the quiz, so apparently they don't care that I overhear what they are saying.

Brazenly, Brittany brags, "I got nineteen out of twenty without even reading."

"So, I got twenty out of twenty, and I didn't read either. I *might* have copied off of someone," Lydia says, laughing, "but I didn't read."

I look up. "Seriously, neither one of you read and you both got As?"

"Yeah," says Lydia. "It's not that hard."

Brittany tries to gauge my reaction and then says, "I just did it because summer reading doesn't really matter. I won't cheat in your class."

Yeah right, I think to myself.

I turn to Allison, whom I had as a freshman. Knowing that she is a voracious reader I ask, "Allison, what did you read over the summer?"

"I read *Of Beetles and Angels, Hamlet*, and then some stuff I wanted."

"How did you do on your summer reading quiz?"

"I took the *Hamlet* quiz because I was curious to see how well I'd do. I didn't do so hot. I missed five, but at least I know where that 'to be or not to be' speech comes from."

Hmm, I think to myself. *Allison reads, challenges herself, doesn't cheat, but ends up penalized with a D as her first grade for the semester. Meanwhile, Brittany and Lydia don't read, don't challenge themselves, and are rewarded with an ill-gotten A for their first grade.* It doesn't seem right that those who know how to cheat or choose not to push themselves end up with higher grades than students who are honest and actually challenge themselves to get smarter. As evidenced by Brittany and Lydia, an A on this quiz doesn't mean they mastered the material.

Granted, giving a multiple-choice test to see who did the summer reading was easy to manage. Unfortunately the grade didn't accurately reflect who read and who didn't. It didn't show who used SparkNotes and who copied from a neighbor. What it did do was invite some kids to play the game of school.

To grade fairly, two factors need to be in place. First, students have to have an opportunity to demonstrate what they understand. Second, the grade has to reflect what the teacher values in terms of content mastery. When the grades I give don't accurately reflect what students know and what I think matters most, I find myself in uncomfortable meetings with disgruntled students and unhappy parents.

Teachers want their students to learn content knowledge and skills, and have a deep understanding of complex concepts. To measure students' progress and guide them to the next level of mastery, I have to use a variety of assessments to gauge what they know. This is where management of the grading becomes important. Multiple-choice tests might be fine for assessing student knowledge, but if I want students to demonstrate more than factual recall, I have to have more complex ways to "see" what they understand. Much of grading depends on how we ask students to show what they know.

Grading critical thinking is messy and hard to calibrate, but teaching students how to critically think, solve problems, and apply the information they learn is vital. Tony Wagner, director of Harvard's Project Zero, notes in his article "Rigor Redefined" (2008) that being able to ask questions and collaborate with others to solve problems are skills that the world outside of school demands. Wagner reports that CEOs, presidents of nonprofits, and military leaders are searching for candidates who can do more than show mastery of basic content knowledge.

In this study, Wagner learned that employers are more than happy to teach employees the factual information they need to be successful on the job. However, taking time to teach potential candidates how to collaborate with colleagues, ask the right questions, and problem solve is too cost prohibitive. Not one employer answered that "factual recall" was a top priority. Wagner reports, "I have yet to talk to a recent graduate, college professor, community leader, or business leader who said that not knowing enough about academic content was a problem" (24).

Unfortunately, factual recall is often measured the most because it is the easiest to grade. When the top consideration for grading is how easily it can be managed, we lose what matters most—understanding and the ability to think critically. During the now infamous era of No Child Left Behind, Washington, DC, officials frequently preached that whatever was tested was emphasized. Students do learn what is emphasized. Unfortunately, what is emphasized is often knowledge that is easy to grade. In many grading and testing cases, what is easy to measure is not necessarily important to know. Understanding is difficult to measure in quantifiable terms. Art Costa, founding director of the Institute for Habits of Mind, has said: "What was educationally significant but hard to measure has been replaced by what is educationally insignificant and easy to measure. So now we measure how well we've taught what isn't worth learning."

How to Think—NOT What to Think

Thinking critically is something that all teachers value and want their students to be able to do. It requires that they know how to construct and convey meaning when the content becomes challenging. To become a successful reader and writer, a student needs to have metacognitive control when it comes to applying thinking strategies. Being able to apply a strategy to repair meaning is an essential skill in every content area. Often teachers ask me how I grade students' use of thinking strategies to make sense of text. Figure 7.1 is a list of long-term learning targets that show what I value about reading and writing. Next to the targets are assessments that students create to show me what they understand.

The following yearlong reading and writing targets are the underpinnings of my subject area. All year we work to achieve mastery in these

Figure 7.1 Learning Targets and Along-the-Way Assessments

Long-Term Learning Target	Assessments
■ Supporting Targets	(Most are graded with points, but not all; see "Beliefs Drive Grading Practices" on page 139 for more information.)
I can demonstrate how reading makes me smarter. ■ I can reread a chunk of text and connect new information to something that I already know. ■ I can make a picture in my head of something I've read in order to remember what I've read. ■ I can use my background knowledge to interpret clues left by the author. ■ I can go beyond the words on the page to infer meaning.	annotated text double-entry diaries inner-voice sheets reading response logs exit tickets journal responses final essays/products/projects that illuminate big content ideas (based on themes, units of study, required texts, etc.)
I can use my discussion group to sustain my reading. ■ I can discuss with my group members to clear up my confusion about a text. ■ I can discuss with my group members to expand my knowledge and understanding of a text.	journal reflections/exit tickets group observation forms scripts of/quotes from group discussions

continued

Figure 7.1 Learning Targets and Along-the-Way Assessments *(continued)*

I can get unstuck and build endurance for reading to get smarter. ■ I can recognize when my mind is wandering. ■ I can reread a chunk of text that I don't understand and ask a question to isolate confusion. ■ I can read for extended periods of time.	response journals exit tickets: what is causing confusion? sticky notes with questions placed in the text where the reading becomes confusing annotated text double-entry diaries inner-voice sheets reading response logs stamina chart (over time) in reading journal
I can get unstuck and build endurance for writing to get smarter. ■ I can increase my writing stamina by producing more than one draft of writing. ■ I can find others who will read my writing and give me useful feedback. ■ I can use published work to mentor my writing. ■ I can show courtesy to my readers by attending to spelling, punctuation, and grammar.	drafts in writing folder revisions and edits on drafts list of editors in writer's journal running list in writer's journal of what I notice other writers doing
I can use writing to demonstrate and clarify my thinking. ■ I can reread what I've written and recognize parts that don't make sense. ■ I can use conferences with my teacher and writing group to revise confusing parts. ■ I can reenter a piece of writing and make changes that reflect how my thinking has evolved.	drafts in writing folders with revisions/annotations exit tickets journal reflections/writing
I can use writing as a way to create awareness and gain access to power in the world. ■ Supporting learning targets vary by project/product.	final products/projects with real-world purpose and audience: ■ 3–5-minute i-movie that creates awareness in peers about a contemporary issue ■ a commentary sent to the local paper stating a position on a local issue ■ an annotated summer reading list ■ book reviews ■ a recommendation to teachers/departments about the use of current works students are reading or should read ■ letters to various organizations/audience

Figure 7.2 Target-Assessment Plan

Workshop Day 1	
Daily/Weekly Learning Targets	**Assessment**
I can show how I am thinking about text in a variety of ways.	inner-voice sheets
Instead of saying, "I don't get it," I can ask a question that might help me build background knowledge that will help me answer my question.	sticky notes

Workshop Day 2	
Daily Learning Targets	**Assessment**
I can select, read, and annotate a piece of nonfiction to build my background knowledge about an area I am curious about.	annotated articles
I can record new learning that I want to share with others.	response journals

areas. However, I need to scaffold learners in order to reach these long-term targets. For this reason, I need to also think about daily and weekly targets that will help me "step" students up to the more sophisticated year-long targets. The daily and weekly targets clearly identify for students what their job is on a day-to-day basis. Figure 7.2 is an example of a daily/weekly target-assessment plan from the workshops I wrote about in Chapter 3. Readers will notice an overlap between my long-term and daily/weekly targets.

Knowing where I'm going makes it easier to ensure that all students get there. When my goal is posted and my assessments are clearly identified, grading describes the journey of *learning* instead of laying judgment on the *learner*.

Grades at the End Aren't Enough

Spending weekends grading is horrible. The only thing that makes those lost weekends worse is having unappreciative students who ignore the written comments. For years, I couldn't figure out why some students wouldn't read what I wrote on their graded assignments. I worked very hard to share information with them so that the next time around they would do a better job. No matter what I wrote, I couldn't get the kids who got Cs, Ds, and Fs, the ones who needed the comments the most, to read what I wrote. One day, Reggie helped me see the light.

Reggie was a senior and a struggling writer. On most days I really liked this kid, but on the days that I returned graded work, Reggie was down-right rude. If he didn't like his grade, he would let out a loud sigh, signaling to the class that his performance was about to begin. He would ceremoniously stand up, stomp to the front of the room, and toss his paper into the air so that it would ever so slowly float down to the waste-basket in the corner. As an encore, he would mutter something under his breath, hoping to catch my eye, so that he could glare at me all the way back to his seat. One day, fed up with his theatrics, I asked him, "Reggie, what's the problem?" When he didn't answer, I said, "You aren't even going to read what I wrote?"

"Nope," he answered.

"And why not?" I asked.

"Look, Ms. T. I know I can't write. I don't need you writing comments all over my paper to tell me I suck."

Feeling a little sorry for him, I explained that I had spent a lot of time grading his paper and that my purpose was not to make him feel bad. "Can't you at least read what I wrote?" I asked.

"Why should I? I worked really hard on that paper, and I still got a bad grade. I don't know how to do it any better."

I explained to Reggie that if he would only read what I wrote, he would know how to write better the next time.

What Reggie asked next stopped me in my tracks. "Can I redo the paper?"

"Why?" I asked.

"So I can get a better grade."

"But I already did all the corrections," I said, and added begrudgingly, "You'll have to do it for homework, because we're moving on to something new today."

"See, Ms. T, that's why I don't read what you write. It's too late to do anything about it."

Since having Reggie as a student, I've changed the way I do things. Had I given him clear learning targets with feedback along the way, Reggie would have become a better writer. Now when I grade final papers and projects, I don't have to make a lot of comments at the end, because I've been doing it along the way. By the time students have turned in their final drafts, they have rewritten and reworked their assignments several times based on the feedback that I've given them. When I do my best job of assessing, students feel pretty good about their learning, and about their grade. They aren't surprised by the final mark because, long before it comes, they have had several chances to apply feedback.

Keeping Students Engaged and Encouraged

Reggie helped me understand that the comments I wrote on his final draft were too late to keep him engaged and encouraged. He helped me realize that students see no point in redoing something that has no relevance. Lastly, he made me see that sometimes I have to grade along the way, in a variety of ways, to keep students engaged in the process.

Varying how I assign points keeps students engaged and allows me flexibility to grade at different stages of the learning process. I can honor students' effort, time, and risks to practice the learning target while they work toward mastery. Students often equate points with success. If something doesn't have points attached to it, they often refuse to engage in the process. With points, I can give them the reinforcement they need to continue practicing. I use three major categories when assigning points: attempt and completion, growth and improvement, and mastery and understanding. Following is a description of each category. I have not included how many points I assign to each category because that will vary from teacher to teacher, based on what they value most.

Points for Attempt and Completion

Students need a chance to practice without someone telling them they are doing it wrong. Unfortunately, it can be quite difficult to get middle and high school learners to do something when points aren't attached. It's even harder to get struggling learners to take a risk when they've been academic failures for years. Many would rather look lazy than stupid.

Because few people improve without practice, I start my year grading for attempt and completion. There are times when I just want students to read or write. To get better at reading and writing, learners need to do it a lot. Without attaching points to the practice time, students may find something else in need of their attention.

When I introduce a new skill, such as annotating, students earn points by practicing. Grading this way gives them an opportunity to figure out how to use the tool and master the skill without worrying about losing points. They have a chance to experiment with the skill, and I don't have to spend a lot of time giving feedback on something they are just practicing. By giving points for attempt and completion, I can encourage risk taking while students get the much-needed practice it takes to master necessary skills.

Example of grading for attempt and completion: Annotate five pieces of thinking on a piece of text. Each piece of thinking is worth three points up to a total of fifteen points.

How this links to what I value: This informs instruction immediately. The teacher can see which students are practicing, what they get, and where their learning needs to be supported.

Points for Growth and Improvement

Practice is important, but I also want students to improve. Students earn points for showing how their thinking is changing and expanding over time—how they are getting smarter, working smarter, and making more meaning. Rubrics, learning targets, and feedback become useful tools that guide students toward exemplary work. On assignments that require multiple drafts, students can earn points for turning in each draft as they continue to refine their work and show growth. Usually I assign twenty-five points for this first attempt. I want to encourage students to start their drafts well before the final deadline. Once students turn in their drafts, I can give them feedback that will guide their second drafts. If students rework the draft using the feedback they've received, they can improve their grades. Students have rubrics and learning targets to guide how their final product will be graded. They can turn in as many drafts as they wish until the final day. Using feedback and learning targets to guide their work improves the quality and cuts down on my final grading at the end.

Example of grading for growth and improvement: Students use feedback from me and from their peers to improve their assignments over time: this could include annotations, reflections, essay drafts, and so on. Students have the learning targets up front and therefore use them to self-assess over time. For this particular type of grading, students have the opportunity to go back and revise and improve their work.

How this links to what I value: Students and teachers work together to improve performance. Teachers can see where differentiation of instruction needs to occur, and students can see their strengths and improve on areas of weakness.

Points for Mastery and Understanding

It is also important to grade for mastery. Both students and I need to know at a particular point what skills, strategies, and understandings they have mastered. However, in many secondary classrooms, learners are graded only on whether or not they "get it." Giving tests and quizzes, and assigning essays and projects, is appropriate as long as students have had an opportunity to practice their learning and get feedback before they are graded for mastery.

Example of grading for mastery: Often these are common assessments, chapter tests, essays, and final projects.

How this links to what I value: These assessments communicate "final" achievement of students on a topic or unit. They help teachers work together to see what instruction was successful—but it does not help current students get smarter if the teacher has moved on to a new topic. This traditional form of grading can inform instruction for the next time the unit is taught.

Beliefs Drive Grading Practices

Grading fairly at the secondary level is difficult. I've been accused of being "too easy." Some mistakenly infer that my low student failure rate is because I have low standards. Other critics complain that letting students have a second chance to rework papers or projects is unfair. To justify my practice, I have to be able to articulate what I believe. These questions help guide my grading practices:

- Should I give students points for engaging in the process of learning?
- How am I using feedback? Is it so students can redo something, or am I just adding comments to defend the grade?
- Am I trying to measure practice, growth, or mastery?
- How do I decide when not to grade something?

To answer these difficult questions, I must make sure that my grading practices are tied to my beliefs about the purpose of education. Four core beliefs guide the way I grade:

Belief #1: Critical thinking matters more than factual recall.

Student thinking matters most. A rigorous curriculum asks students to think every day. A rigorous teacher asks students to leave evidence of their thinking every day so growth can be measured over time.

Belief #2: Risk, struggle, practice, and success are essential to learning.

If I want students to take risks, struggle through difficulty, and practice skills, the work needs to be worth their time. Students need reinforcement along the way, in the form of individual attention, feedback, and points, to nudge them toward success.

Belief #3: Smart is something you become.

Grades should not be used as a fixed label—Johnny cannot be a C student in everything at all times. Grades should reflect a student's current understanding. Because I'm most concerned about students getting smarter and more skillful each day, I don't want a poor grade earned at the beginning of the quarter to penalize a student for the entire semester.

Belief #4: The world is an interesting place. The more my classroom mirrors the world, the more engaged students will be.

I plan what I want students to be able to do at the end of the unit to ensure that each day my students and I are working toward that goal. By helping them create rich, authentic products and projects, they will have an impetus to work hard.

Bullies, Barriers, and Bad Policies

Sometimes people question my judgment and wonder why I so readily accept late work. I know that students have complex, full lives outside of school. It is easy to forget that they are as stressed out as we are. When it comes to grading, I have to remember that their learning takes precedence over my organizational rules and regulations. In many classrooms around the country, students flunk or do poorly because they have turned work in late. I always accept late work because I value their learning more than my deadline. Not all readers will agree with this premise, but I ask that they think about why accepting late work is not permissible. Consider the following stories.

Attending my daughter's freshman back-to-school night, I am surprised that many of her teachers don't accept late work. No excuses. Period. Assignments turned in late receive an F. I am struck by the rigidity of the policy and wonder if it is more for the convenience of the teacher than for the benefit of the students. Each teacher's explanation for their unwavering commitment to timeliness connects to their theory that they are "making students responsible." In all honesty, I'd prefer to teach responsibility to my daughter rather than leaving it up to the twenty-three-year-old algebra teacher with the tattoo peeking out from her midriff. Personal feelings aside, life sometimes gets in the way, and occasionally even very responsible adults miss deadlines.

Sometimes, pressure from colleagues to not accept late work forces me to reconsider my position. However, thinking of Tommy reminds me why I started accepting late work in the first place. Several years ago the English department was embroiled in a conversation about a department-wide late-work policy. After the meeting, Tommy's English teacher stopped me in the hall. With consternation in her voice, she told me that our differing policies were confusing him. She was concerned that my lenient stance was giving him the wrong message. "When you let Tommy turn in work late" she said, "it sends the message that it is okay to be irresponsible."

Surprised by her stance, I asked, "Do you have any idea how difficult Tommy's life is outside of school?"

Undaunted, she said, "A difficult life outside of school is all the more reason to teach him responsibility."

"What makes you think Tommy isn't responsible?" I asked.

Without missing a beat, she answered, "Responsible kids care about school, and they show it by turning their work in on time."

My colleague's presumptive attitude put me on the defensive. I shared with her just how "irresponsible" Tommy was. Tommy is the oldest of three. His mom had a drinking problem and struggled to take care of the younger children. At night, Tommy tried to make sure the kids were fed and bathed. In the mornings, he got them up, fed them breakfast, and walked them to school. Some mornings went more smoothly than others. On days when things didn't go well, Tommy was late to school and usually didn't have his homework done. He accepted his detentions, his Fs, and his teacher's insensitive remarks because in his mind, taking care of his younger brother and sister was the responsible thing to do.

I couldn't tell from my colleague's expression whether she got the connection. However, the morning bell was about to ring, so I headed for class.

Tommy's English teacher was being hardnosed about his homework because she didn't know him as a learner. Tommy's pride prevented him from explaining his circumstances. Thanks to the conversation calendars, I got to know Tommy better than most of his teachers. Writing short notes on his calendar was a safe way for him to let me know what was going on in his life and what was keeping him from being successful. Knowing Tommy not only as a learner but as a person allowed me to modify my instruction so I could better meet his needs.

Tommy's English class met after my reading class. Knowing his struggles, I could sometimes carve out time for him to do his English homework. I got him a planner, and we looked for spaces during the day when he could squeeze in some homework. By second quarter, Tommy was learning how to manage his time and able to meet most of his English deadlines.

When we don't know our students well, we have no way of knowing what is preventing them from being successful. Accepting late work when other teachers don't is inconsistent, but in the long run, homework is not what matters most. Tommy needed some coaching on how to balance all of his responsibilities. He had figured out long ago what it meant to be responsible. He didn't need weekly deadlines to teach him that. Deadlines alone don't have the power to make people responsible. More often than not, they only add stress to people's lives.

Accepting or not accepting late work is not the issue. It is more important to find out what is preventing kids from doing the work in the first place. Most students want to be successful, so when they aren't, it's my job to find out why. I ask these questions:

- Have I done the assignment myself? What hurdles did I face that my students might be experiencing?
- Have I modeled how to negotiate the hurdles?
- Is the assignment boring? Is it too hard? Is it busywork?
- Have I articulated a clear purpose for the assignment? Have I defined clear criteria of what will be graded?
- How will students who need more help access me? Is the reading material too hard? Is it easier on students' pride to appear lazy than to appear stupid?
- Are there extenuating circumstances beyond a student's control that prevent him or her from doing the work?

Few things in life are black or white. Having empathy for Tommy and letting him turn in work late doesn't equate to low standards. It acknowledges that school, like life, is challenging and that it is more important to know how to negotiate those challenges than to give up or cheat in order to "play the game of school." Sure, I accepted his late work, but I also tried to show him some strategies for managing his time. Thinking beyond the grade itself helps me balance policies with what is best for kids. Had I not been able to articulate my beliefs about grading, I would have fallen into the trap that the world is black and white instead of helping Tommy see that the world is full of shades of gray.

Hard Versus Rigorous

Grades should not be used to reward and punish student behavior, attendance, or study habits. Years ago, I mediated a conversation between Julia, a struggling reader; her mom, a health care worker; and Mr. C., her U.S. history teacher. Julia was working hard, but the amount of content that the class was supposed to learn was daunting. The teacher prided himself on his high failure rate and even went so far as to say that at this point in the semester it wasn't unusual for more than 70 percent of his freshmen to be failing. He paused, looked at Julia's mom, and said, "Don't worry, this happens to most freshmen until they figure out that high school is a lot more rigorous than middle school."

Sensing the mother's frustration, I wasn't quite sure how I was going to mediate the conversation. I felt sorry for Julia and wondered how I could support her when it came to reading the social studies text. Not noticing the mother's ire, Mr. C. continued, "Until students decide to put forth more effort, there is nothing I can do."

Before I could get a word in edgewise, the mom held up her hand, leaned toward the social studies teacher, and through clenched teeth, quietly said, "I work in the health care field, and if my patients had a seventy percent failure rate, not only would I not be bragging about it, but I'd be out of a job." We were all silent. She was right. If a 70 percent failure rate is unacceptable in the real world, why would it be considered "rigorous" in school?

Often educators equate rigor with high expectations. Teachers are told that if they set the bar high, students will rise to it. This is true only when expectations are reasonable and sufficient scaffolding is provided. When they aren't realistic and students are expected to "jump" to meet the bar, they experience failure and frustration, and ultimately quit. Simply setting a high bar isn't enough when there are no rungs on the ladder, supporting a student's climb.

The word *rigor* is being thrown around a lot these days. Just last spring, a high school English coordinator called to ask me if I thought reading six novels in a year was too much. I asked why he wanted to know, and he said he'd had a pretty heated discussion with one of his English teachers. Apparently, she had taken one of my classes and I had given her the impression that reading six books was too much. The teacher was struggling with the amount of literature she needed to teach, and because her students were struggling readers, many of the texts were too hard. She reasoned that if she had one less book to teach, students would have more time to construct meaning.

I asked the department chair what texts students were expected to read. In a defensive tone, he said the works weren't that long or hard, and then rattled off the following titles: *Julius Caesar, Catcher in the Rye, The Great Gatsby, The Things They Carried, Of Mice and Men*, and *A Separate Peace*.

True, by English teacher standards, these titles aren't long or hard, especially if the teacher has taught them for several years. However, for the average fifteen-year-old, these works can be challenging. After he finished listing the titles, I asked him what he wanted to observe when visiting classrooms. "I want to see students reading, writing, and discussing," he said. "I want to see critical thinking going on."

"Is that what you are seeing now?" I asked.

"No, I don't see that at all. That's one reason why I don't want this teacher to drop any of the required texts. I think she needs to ramp up the rigor."

Rigor again. "Do you think if there weren't so many novels to teach, the students would have more time to read, write, and think critically?" I asked.

There was a pause on the other end of the phone. I pleaded the teacher's case, reminding him that young readers don't just pick up classic works of literature and automatically comprehend them. They need time and opportunities to read, write, and discuss the literature to engage in critical thinking. If teachers don't have to cover so many works of literature, students will have more time to do the work.

At this point in the conversation, I could tell he was getting frustrated, and I was getting bored. He had figured out that I wasn't going to support him in his quest to cover the amount of literature he thought was important, and I had accepted that the teacher wasn't going to be allowed to lighten her content load. As our conversation drew to an end, he asked me what tenth graders in my building read. I shared the anchor texts (*Things They Carried, The Great Gatsby, Julius Caesar*) and waited for his response. There was silence on his end of the phone. Finally he let out a sigh and said, "Well, I guess I just want more rigor for my department than you want for yours." With that he thanked me for my time and hung up.

The department chair's comment stung and rolled around in my head all summer long. All teachers want their instruction to be rigorous. No one wants to look like a slacker. In the field of education, the words *rigorous* and *hard* are often used synonymously. For me, the two terms have vastly different meanings. Curious to see if other teachers agreed, I interviewed several and asked them to think about something they had recently read that was challenging. I then asked them to name what about the reading made it hard. Teachers shared how much they detested reading certain texts. They referred to bank documents, legal forms, maps, directions, and diagrams. When they told me what made the reading difficult, I began to list the barriers. The most common responses were as follows:

Reading is hard when . . .
- I don't have background knowledge about the topic.
- I have to come up with the "right" answer.
- There are too many details.
- There are not enough details.
- The font is small.
- I don't know the vocabulary or key terms.
- I can't see a purpose for the reading or how it's relevant to my life.
- I'm stressed or have a problem on my mind.
- There are lots of pages to read and there is not enough time to do it.
- I have no choice in what I read.
- There are no diagrams or illustrations.
- I'm tired.
- I don't care about the topic.

As I compare the terms *hard* and *rigorous*, I don't think we want hard for our students. Ironically the very same qualities on the list above that make reading hard for adults also make reading hard for students. As adults we tend to avoid hard, so why in the world would we think students wouldn't do the same? We must ask ourselves, *Do we want school to be hard for our students, or do we want it to be rigorous?* Assuming rigor is intended to be a positive outcome of good instruction, how do we distinguish it from just plain hard?

Hard Hurts; Rigor Invigorates

I avoid hard. Hard is discouraging because I seldom experience success. Rigor, on the other hand, is something I embrace. When a task is rigorous, I keep coming back for more. I can sustain my engagement over a period of time because I've achieved success along the way and I see progress. I am encouraged by my accomplishments, so I push myself to take more risks. As I get better at the task, I can take on a greater degree of difficulty. When things are hard, I don't reach my destination no matter how determined I am.

Rigor is not a set standard. It changes, depending on a learner's skill and motivation.

To test this theory, I consider what rigor is outside the realm of school. Two years ago, I decided to get into shape. My left knee hurt so badly that I could no longer get out of my car without a shooting pain coursing through my leg. Skiing was out of the question, as everyday movements were a chore. Deciding to get my knee replaced, I asked my colleague Wade to recommend a surgeon. Wade teaches physical education and is a former professional football player. If anyone could recommend a good orthopedic surgeon, it would be him. I trusted Wade, and when he told me that I didn't need an orthopedic surgeon, I needed to lose twenty pounds and while I was at it, start exercising, I was taken aback. I wanted a quick fix. At the time, I didn't know my friend had given me the best advice I could have received.

Begrudgingly, I asked Wade how I should begin. He said, "Start by walking twenty minutes a day until you can walk a mile. Once you get to the mile, increase the time and the speed. Work up to thirty minutes a day and see if you can walk more distance each day in less time. Shoot for a fifteen-minute mile."

When I began, a fifteen-minute mile was out of the question. For me walking twenty minutes without stopping was a rigorous workout. I had to push myself. I got sweaty. I was sore, but it was a good sore. Best of all, I kept at it. Each week I could feel myself getting stronger, so I walked longer and faster. Two years later, I'm doing three miles in the time it took me to walk one.

When I share this story with young people who are in shape, they scoff. "A fifteen-minute mile? Why bother?" they say. For them, it isn't even exercise. However, for older friends who are less in shape, this is overdoing it. It finally hit me. Rigor for one is not rigor for all. It is not a single fixed bar placed high above the class. Rather there are different bars set at multiple levels, depending on individual needs and capabilities. The bar is set just high enough so that each student can grab on with just the right amount of scaffolding and modeling.

Many teachers helped me think through the differences between hard and rigorous. Figure 7.3 identifies how the two terms differ.

A principal once asked me, "Can a remedial reading class by rigorous?" My response was, "It better be." I wondered if she had confused rigorous with hard.

Figure 7.3 The Differences Between Hard and Rigorous in the World Outside of School

Hard	Rigorous
Learners avoid hard tasks.	Learners embrace rigorous tasks.
The goal is the same for everyone no matter what their starting place is.	The goal changes as learners achieve small successes. With each success, a new goal is set.
Lack of success discourages learners.	Small successes keep the learners coming back for more.
Someone or something other than the learner is in control of the process and the timetable for success.	Learners have control over the process and also determine how quickly they progress.
Expectations are unreasonable because they are not set by the learner, but by outsiders who maintain control.	Expectations are set by the learner, and because the expectation is realistic, the learner sticks with the task.
Learners are frustrated because they lack tools and strategies to access the task.	Learners are empowered because they have tools and strategies to access the task.
Learners need outside prodding or extrinsic rewards to engage.	Learners prod themselves because intrinsic rewards drive them to engage.
Learners don't see a need for the task because it has no immediate relevance to their life.	Learners recognize a need for the learning and see a purpose for the work.
Compliance takes place because the performance of the task is done for someone else.	Engagement takes place because learning is for the individual.

I explained that the level of rigor is set by the needs of the learner. The teacher must work to find the appropriate level of challenge for each student. It isn't about the number of novels or the number of pages a teacher assigns. It's not about how quickly she blasts through content or how hard she grades. Rigor varies from learner to learner. When a large number of students are failing a class, teachers need to consider if they are confusing rigorous with hard.

Mandates brought on by No Child Left Behind have changed the rules of the game. In the past, teachers could hide behind rigor by saying, "Here is what I expect. If you can't meet this expectation, drop the class." Now, teachers are required to move all students forward regardless of their skill level. When teachers determine what rigor is, they must consider the needs of each student. Rigor can no longer be relegated to the honors courses. Differentiated rigor is something all learners deserve, and grading practices have to reflect this.

Teachers who aren't intentional about their grading practices are easy marks for criticism. No one wants to be accused of being a bully who puts up barriers trying to defend bad policies. In this day and age of scrutiny, we need to know why we grade the way we do and be able to communicate it clearly to students, parents, and administrators. When grades reflect what teachers value, and students know what they're being graded on and why and how they're being graded, they will engage.

What Works

Assessment Point: Effective assessors brainstorm and plan what they want students to know and be able to do before they begin a unit. They know that daily instructional moves are based on what they see and hear students do on a daily basis. Effective assessors don't wait for the chapter test to see if students have mastered the material. They assess along the way. When teachers have a destination in mind, they can give more time and attention to students.

Assessment Point: Assessments are most powerful when learners can use the information to help themselves—they know what their grades represent. When students begin to "self-assess," they can ask for help and teachers can adjust their practices to better meet their needs. When students are in control of their own learning, they stop playing the game of school and begin to work for understanding, rather than an isolated score, as their goal.

"Are You Up for a Challenge?"

1. Take the time to chart out what you want students to be able to do at the end of a grading period. Create a long-term plan. Knowing what you want students to know and do at the end of the unit gives you a road map with which to build daily lessons. After you have a goal in mind, think about the steps or learning targets students will need to meet to reach the goal. During work time, let kids create evidence of learning. Think about the tracks of thinking they will leave for you to assess. Know that not everything has to be graded. Remember, your job is to uncover understanding, not cover content.

2. Don't grade everything. If you do, students will stop taking risks. Instead, honor their time and effort by giving them attempt-and-completion points. Use work time to provide feedback so that you can grade their growth. Consider what content, skills, or strategies you are assessing so both you and students are clear on what mastery looks like. Make grading manageable.

Coda: Break the Fake

Growth reports, annual yearly progress, and target gains—the urgent talk of assessment is everywhere. Sometimes in a frenzy the discussions drift so far away from the classroom that students and teachers are left out of the conversation. Schools are inundated with nonstop assessment and data collection, and educators must remind themselves why they are assessing in the first place. When it comes to assessment, my bottom line rests with being able to answer the following three questions:

- How are students progressing?
- What do they need next?
- How do I plan my instruction to get students to the next level?

Assessment is what we make it. If we expand our definition and consider how we use it to our advantage, we don't have to breathlessly await state test results in hopes that our students showed growth. We can take matters into our own hands if we are willing to include and use what we see and hear in our classrooms every day as data. Sometimes the data is serendipitous and we discover an artifact that we initially don't recognize as worthwhile. Yet, with an open mind, it could have the potential to inform our teaching more than any test results we receive.

Remember Faraz and the multiple-choice vocabulary test? The information gleaned from the use of his cell phone during the vocabulary test was disappointing. But the realization that he, like many kids, would go to great lengths to survive an assessment forced me to examine my instructional practice. It led me to learning targets and thinking about how I could use the workshop model to "assess" and instruct students all period long. I knew I had to "break the fake," not only for students but for myself, when it came to relying on summative assessments to tell me how we were progressing.

Several years ago, I started giving my cell-phone number out to students. When I was on the road, I wanted them to have access to me if they got stuck. At first, I worried that I would get nonstop phone calls at all hours of the day. I quickly realized that students were too busy to chat. Instead they efficiently text-message me whenever they need something. Sometimes I get texts that ask me what page in their novel they should be on. Other times they text to find out if I can meet them before school to help them with an assignment. The best ones allow me a quick peek into their thinking. The series of texts that I got from Kai gave me a whole new appreciation for formative assessments.

5:33:31 PM Nov 16

Kai: This is Kai . . . so i.ve been reading gatsby and it is mak.n me really mad. Why is he standing by daisy? Why is he will.n to take the fall for her . . . why would he risk get.n in trouble and possibly go.n to jail? She is the one that hit and killed Myrtle not him.

7:46:23 PM Nov 16

Me: I know! Daisy is so selfish. Gatsby lived his whole life to "get" her. He was willing to do whatever it took to attain his dream. Was it worth it? BTW—I'm so proud of you for reading.

7:50:34 PM Nov 16

Kai: So now I'm on the part where Gatsby tells nick about how he was accidentally sent to oxford and I'm just get.n so mad that G still loves her—I don't even want to read anymore. He made me SOO mad.

7:53:48 PM Nov 16

Me: Keep reading. It gets worse. Do you think he is a wuss?

8:00:32 PM Nov 16

Kai: Do I think who is a wuss? And I know it gets worse. I stop.d at the part where Gatsby said in any case it was personal.

8:31:07 PM Nov 16

Me: Sorry. Do you think Nick is a wuss? Why doesn't he speak up for Gatsby? They are all chickens.

8:35:31 PM Nov 16

Kai: I really think nick is a wuss. I was extremely mad when nick didn't say anything about tom cheat.n . . . and I've noticed that the further you read, there are lots more colors mention.d

Green, yellow, and the rim is blue although I don't think the blue matters.

9:35:54 PM Nov 16

Me: Has the color red come up yet?

9:37:42 PM Nov 16

Kai: Nope not yet but more than likely I will finish the book 2mrow and the way everything is going I'm almost positive it will come up soon.

9:52:23 PM Nov 16

Me: Don't tell people how the book ends. K?

9:53:41 PM Nov 16

Kai: Okay I won't. lolx

10:00:00 PM Nov 16

Me: thanks

Teaching on a block schedule means that sometimes I don't see students for three days in a row. If we have class on Thursday, I don't see students until the following Monday. So the next evening, I get another text from Kai:

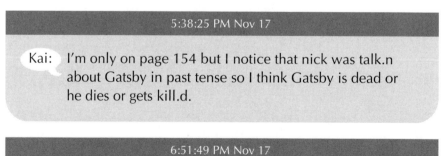

5:38:25 PM Nov 17

Kai: I'm only on page 154 but I notice that nick was talk.n about Gatsby in past tense so I think Gatsby is dead or he dies or gets kill.d.

6:51:49 PM Nov 17

Kai: p162 the color red shows up. I dont thnk it's a coincidence that tom & daisy leave hours b4 gatsby is kill.d & leave no contact info . . . I think they were afraid they'd get caught.

Over a two-day period, Kai and I texted back and forth, sharing thoughts about *The Great Gatsby*. In awe, I realize that the amount of assessment data from these short snippets of conversation yield more information than any test I could buy or design. From Kai's texts, I learn a lot about her as a reader. More important, I gain insight into her as a person. I can tell by her disgust that Fitzgerald has struck a chord. Like thousands of readers before her, she feels Gatsby's disillusionment. I learn that she can go beyond plot using a literary element to track another facet of literature. She follows Fitzgerald's use of color and connects it to symbolic meaning. She looks for textual evidence to guide her predictions. Kai notices the change in verb tense and uses it to infer the ending. Even though she struggles with the vocabulary and some of the long descriptions, she is tenacious in her quest to finish the book. I can tell by her texts that she feels privileged to be in on the author's "hidden meaning."

When I look at the formative assessment data I've collected from students, and reflect on all that it tells me, I don't have to give a summative test to see who read the book and who didn't. I can tell from students' annotations, their reading journals, my conferring notes, and even their text messages what they have learned and how they have improved. These formative assessments not only show my students and me growth over time, but also help us know where to go next.

For years I have told students to be selfish readers, to make sure that every time they read they get a little smarter. Happily, I realize that I have become a selfish assessor. From the summative assessments that I gave Faraz's class to see if test scores matched my estimation of their progress, to Kai's indignant response to *The Great Gatsby*, I recognize that every day I have a chance to get smarter about instruction and student growth. There are all kinds of ways to "break the fake" and discover what students truly know. With this new focus, I am able to embrace assessment and let it guide my instruction to help me better serve my students. Students get smarter, and so do I. No need to fake it.

Appendix

Name _____

Period _____

Date _____

INNER-VOICE SHEET

Title of Book _____

Author of Book _____

Directions: Begin reading on page _____. Record the conversation you have in your head as you read. Be sure to have at least four (4) sentences per box. If you catch yourself using a reading strategy, add that at the bottom of the box. Also decide if the conversation inside your head distracts you from making meaning or if the voice helps you interact with the text.

Inner Voice on page	Inner Voice on page
Inner Voice on page	**Inner Voice on page**

Conversation Calendar
(Monday, Wednesday, Friday)

Name:

Period:

Week of:

Monday	Wednesday	Friday

Conversation Calendar
(Tuesday, Thursday)

Name:

Period:

Week of:

Tuesday	Thursday

Conversation Calendar
(Monday–Friday)

Name:

Period:

Week of:

Monday	Tuesday	Wednesday	Thursday	Friday
☐	☐	☐	☐	☐
☐	☐	☐	☐	☐

References

Albom, M. 2003. *The Five People You Meet in Heaven*. New York: Hyperion.

Alexie, Sherman. 2007. *The Absolutely True Diary of a Part-Time Indian*. New York: Little, Brown.

Allen, P. 2009. *Conferring: The Keystone of Reader's Workshop*. Portland, ME: Stenhouse.

Allington, R. L. 2001. *What Really Matters for Struggling Readers*. New York: Addison Wesley Longman.

Anderson, C. 2000. *How's It Going?: A Practical Guide to Conferring with Student Writers*. Portsmouth, NH: Heinemann.

Annas, G. J., and M. A. Grodin. 1992. *The Nazi Doctors and the Nuremberg Code: Human Rights in Human Experimentation*. New York: Oxford University Press.

Anonymous. 2005. *Go Ask Alice*. New York: Simon Pulse.

Asgedom, M. 2002. *Of Beetles and Angels: A Boy's Remarkable Journey from a Refugee Camp to Harvard*. New York: Little, Brown Books for Young Readers.

Atwell, N. 1998. *In the Middle: New Understandings about Writing, Reading, and Learning*. Portsmouth, NH: Heinemann.

Bennett, S. 2007. *That Workshop Book: New Systems and Structures for Classrooms That Read, Write, and Think*. Portsmouth, NH: Heinemann.

Black, P., and D. Wiliam. 1998. "Inside the Black Box: Raising Standards through Classroom Assessment." *Phi Delta Kappan* 80 (2): 139–144, 146–148.

Conley, D. 2005. *College Knowledge: What It Really Takes for Students to Succeed and What We Can Do to Get Them Ready*. San Francisco: Jossey-Bass.

Earl, L. 2003. *Assessment as Learning: Using Classroom Assessment to Maximize Student Learning*. Thousand Oaks, CA: Corwin.

Elmore, R. F. 2000. *Building a New Structure for School Leadership*. Washington, DC: Albert Shanker Institute.

Fitzgerald, F. S. 1999. *The Great Gatsby*. New York: Scribner.

Frey, J. 1995. *A Million Little Pieces*. New York: Anchor.

Graves, D. 1983. *Writing: Teachers and Children at Work*. Portsmouth, NH: Heinemann.

———. 2001. *The Energy to Teach*. Portsmouth, NH: Heinemann.

Hakim, J. 2003. *The History of US*. New York: Oxford University Press.

Harvard College Library. 2007. "Interrogating Texts: Six Reading Habits to Develop in Your First Year at Harvard." Harvard University. http://hcl.harvard.edu/research/guides/lamont_handouts/interrogatingtexts.html.

Hobbs, Will. 2006. *Crossing the Wire*. New York: Harper Trophy.

Hunter, A., D. Joseph, and J. LaHunt. 2004. *Around the Way Girls*. New York: Urban Books.

Knowles, J. 2003. *A Separate Peace*. New York: Scribner.

Marzano, R. J. 2003. *What Works in Schools: Translating Research into Action*. Alexandria, VA: Association for Supervision and Curriculum Development.

Moss, C., and S. Brookhart. 2009. *Advancing Formative Assessment in Every Classroom: A Guide for Instructional Leaders*. Alexandria, VA: ASCD.

O'Brien, T. 2009. *The Things They Carried*. New York: Mariner Books.

Orwell, G. 2003. *1984*. New York: Plume.

Peltzer, D. 1995. *A Child Called It: One Child's Courage to Survive*. New York: Health Communications.

Reeves, D. B. 2000. *Accountability in Action: A Blueprint for Learning Organizations*. Denver: Advanced Learning Press.

———. 2004. *Accountability for Learning: How School Leaders and Teachers Can Take Charge*. Alexandria, VA: Association for Supervision and Curriculum Development.

Rodriguez, S., and R. Sanchez. 2008. *Lady Q: The Rise and Fall of a Latin Queen*. Chicago: Chicago Review Press.

Salinger, J. D. 1951. *Catcher in the Rye*. New York: Little, Brown.

Schmoker, M. 2006. *Results Now: How We Can Achieve Unprecedented Improvements in Teaching and Learning*. Alexandria, VA: Association for Supervision and Curriculum Development.

———. 2009. "What Money Can't Buy: Powerful, Overlooked Opportunities for Learning." *Phi Delta Kappan* 90 (7): 524–527.

Shakespeare, W. 2003. *Hamlet*. New York: Simon and Schuster.

———. 2005. *Julius Caesar*. New York: Simon and Schuster.

Simpson, C. 2006. *Inside the Crips: Life Inside L.A.'s Most Notorious Gang*. New York: St. Martin's Griffin.

Steinbeck, J. 2002. *Of Mice and Men*. New York: Penguin.

Stiggins, R., J. A. Arter, J. Chappuis, and S. Chappuis. 2004. *Classroom Assessment for Student Learning: Doing It Right, Using It Well*. Portland, OR: Assessment Training Institute.

Tovani, C. 2000. *I Read It, but I Don't Get It*. Portland, ME: Stenhouse.

———. 2004. *Do I Really Have to Teach Reading?* Portland, ME: Stenhouse.

Venkatesh, S. 2008. *Gang Leader for a Day: A Rogue Sociologist Takes to the Streets*. New York: Penguin.

Wagner, T. 2008. "Rigor Redefined." *Education Leadership* 60 (2): 20–25.

Wiesenthal, S. 1998. *The Sunflower*. New York: Schocken.

Wiggins, G., and J. McTighe. 2005. *Understanding by Design*. Expanded 2nd ed. Alexandria, VA: Association for Supervision and Curriculum Development.

Yeats, J. B. 1946. *Letters to His Son W. B. Yeats and Others, 1869–1922*. New York: Dutton.

Zemelman, S., H. Daniels, and D. Hyde. 1998. *Best Practice: New Standards for Teaching and Learning in America's Schools*. Portsmouth, NH: Heinemann.